A MANUAL OF STRUCTURED EXPERIENCES FOR CROSS-CULTURAL LEARNING

William H. Weeks

Paul B. Pedersen

Richard W. Brislin

Editors

The International Society for
Intercultural Education, Training and Research

Intercultural Press Inc.

Published by Intercultural Press, Inc.
P.O. Box 768
Yarmouth, Maine 04096

Library of Congress Catalogue Card Number 79-100422
ISBN 0-933662-05-X

Printed in the United States of America

ACKNOWLEDGEMENTS

Many of the structured learning experiences in this volume have had a long tradition in sundry use and, during this process, their exact origins have become obscured. Changes have been made by various people, and these exercises have undergone modifications for this volume so that they conform to a cross-cultural framework. In an effort to preserve knowledge about an exercise's origin and to extend our appreciation to those who contributed to this volume, we have endeavored to trace the geneology of specific structured experiences and acknowledge those persons and organizations responsible for their development and for the overall development of this publication. Unfortunately, we have probably been unsuccessful in our attempts to credit all of the persons and settings that have had input in the development of the following exercises. We apologize for unintended omissions in this regard.

A large number of the exercises presented in this volume originated with the Peace Corps as a product of the experience and creativity of Peace Corp's training staff and returning overseas volunteers. We would like to thank in particular Albert R. Wight and Mary Ann Hammons, editors of *Guidelines for Peace Corps Cross-Cultural Training*.

The United Nations' Educational, Scientific, and Cultural Organization (UNESCO) has developed many original exercises and has adapted structured experiences for their cross-cultural training purposes. We are especially indebted to Professor Sidney Simon of the University of Massachusetts, and Henry Holmes and Stephen Guild, editors of *A Manual of Teaching Techniques for Intercultural Education*. We are grateful also to the Department of the Navy Personnel Research and Development Center, and R. Garry Shirts of Simile II for sharing their expertise in the area of cross-cultural simulation.

Dr. Royal Freuhling of the Educational Foundations Department, University of Hawaii, provided the editors with several materials pertaining to cross-cultural communication and much thoughtful guidance in their adaptation and use.

Peter S. Adler, Orientation Officer at Hawaii's East-West Center also supplied the editors with valuable source materials and publication suggestions.

We are further indebted to Miss Penny Paik for helping us trace the origins of several structured experiences and guiding us to useful source materials.

Finally, we would like to thank Joy Ichiyama for her assistance in preparing permission requests and manuscript sections without which certain publication deadlines could not have been met.

William W. Weeks
Paul B. Pedersen
Richard W. Brislin

iv

TABLE OF CONTENTS

PROS AND CONS OF USING STRUCTURED EXERCISES IN INTERCULTURAL GROUPS

by Paul Pedersen and William Howell

Every group is "intercultural" to the extant that members make different assumptions and value different goals as being most important. Groups where these value differences are most obvious, as in multinational or ethnic groups, are more likely to accommodate the value differences into the ways they all come from the same nationality or ethnic group. Subtle value differences have a potential for being overlooked and, to that extent, are perhaps even more likely to affect the outcome of a group than the more obvious cultural differences.

Each value orientation places its own restrictions on what is and what is not appropriate. In some groups the members may place a premium on frankness, openness and free expression of feelings, which have been associated with human relations training, while in other groups these very same behaviors might be considered offensive. For example, what should a facilitator do with a "silent" member from another culture? Perhaps the facilitator needs to be more aware of non-verbal communication especially by persons from cultures which place less emphasis on verbalization. A special difficulty of intercultural groups is the expectation that behaviors considered desirable by some members will almost certainly be considered undesirable by others. In addition to the value orientations of participants, the exercise or structure or procedure being used by the group brings perhaps still another value orientation with it; and finally, the setting or environment in which the group is meeting imposes its own assumptions of value orientation!

Research on the "contact hypothesis" has demonstrated that merely getting members of different groups together is not enough to produce understanding and harmony except under especially "favorable" conditions. Favorable conditions imply equal status contact between members of the different groups: when contact occurs between members of the majority group and higher status members of a minority group, when the social climate promotes harmony, when the contact is intimate rather than casual, when the contact is pleasant or rewarding and when members of all groups are working toward superordinate goals.

Social exchange theory assumes that the positive or negative consequences of intercultural exchange depend on how pleasurable or satisfying the contact becomes. For example, no participant should be forced to participate in a group exercise because non-voluntary involvement is almost certain to result in bad feelings. Frustration will reduce the favorableness of intercultural contact even when neither side is at fault. In the same way pleasure will be generalized through a "halo" effect to increase the favorableness of contact. However, what is pleasurable to one person might be frustrating to another. The condition of "favorable contact" is not likely to occur spontaneously and will require some structured guidance by leaders of participating groups.

Attempts to design "culture free" group procedures have not been successful, or even desirable for that matter, given the intercultural complexity of most groups. Attempts to identify and specify the value assumptions of the members, the leader, the exercise and the setting have helped participants to understand one another better. Even being open about one's assumptions can impose its own values on an unwilling participant so that the larger responsibility for cultural sensitivity rests on the participants and particularly on the group leader in perceiving and appropriately accommodating the values of participants in an intercultural group. Finally, the appropriateness of interaction in a group depends on how participants are guided to relate toward one another. Almost any exercise or procedure has a potential for helping an intercultural group, even though the exercise was not originally designed to get at cultural values at all.

The structured experiences for cross-cultural learning have been either adapted from other popular exercises to emphasize value differences, or they have been designed within intercultural groups to meet a particular need at a particular time. Each intercultural facilitator has developed and designed favorites that work for him or her even though others might try the same procedure unsuccessfully. These previously unpublished structures might suggest adaptations for intercultural facilitators to complement their own collection of structures and intercultural resources. Each reader will no doubt find some more appropriate than others for his or her particular setting. They were selected from a large number of fugitive exercises, including those approaches that are adaptable to a variety of cultural value orientations and not exclusively or rigidly representing a particular culture. In all of them, the group leader must be sensitive to how this structure places a participant in an embarrassing situation or otherwise violates the value orientation of a group member. The group leader has an ethical obligation not to impose his or her values through any structure in an attempt to manipulate the group participants against their will. Even the most sensitive group leader will no doubt represent a particular value orientation as a result of his or her own cultural socialization, but it should be represented in a way that will help the group move toward its defined goals.

x

The first cluster of structures emphasizes ways of introducing participants to one another, suggesting both more direct methods such as introducing yourself to another culture, or less direct approaches such as telling about the group as though the session had already been completed. These three structures suggest some alternatives on getting a group started by getting them to know more about one another.

The second cluster of structures demonstrates the dynamics of communication processes. They are either tightly controlled, such as "Following Directions" and "Cross-Cultural Trade-Off," or more open-ended, such as "Rumor Transmission" and the use of taped excerpts from group interaction. The more ambiguous a communication exercise, the more skill is required by a group leader in appropriately applying the structure. At any point these exercises might reveal some important insight to the group and the group may abandon the structure and concentrate on the insight. The danger is that a structure might become more important than the insights it reveals. The trick is to keep that from occurring!

The third cluster of structures attempts to help a group clarify value differences. Some of these structures are related to the content of the discussion, such as "Critical Incidents," "Case Studies," "Value Statements Exercise," or the "Implicit Assumptions Checklist." Others are directed toward the process of working together, such as "The Parable," "Letters to the Editors," "Policy Statements," or generating "Cultural Value Systems with Conflicting Points of View." Still others are ambiguous, such as the "Free Drawing" and "Comparing People to Objects" approaches, which might result in surprising insights from the perspective of either content or process of value orientations. The more ambiguous and projective structures again will require a higher level of skill or training to be applied appropriately. When structures are used inappropriately, they may confuse rather than clarify knowledge about a participant's value orientation.

A fourth cluster deals with role identification within an intercultural group. Some of these structures require participants to role play in front of a group. This might be offensive to some more than others. These structures require the direct involvement of a participant, as in "The Situation Exercise," the "Orientation for a Cross-Cultural Experience," and the other three role playing exercises. To some extent "The Hidden Agenda" also requires that participants role play someone other than themselves. Other structures analyze the role relationships within a group, such as "The Fish Bowl," "Projecting into a Group," the "Personal Role Model" and the "Marital Roles Scale." This less direct involvement is probably less threatening to most participants and leads easily toward discussion about role identification.

A fifth cluster evaluates group processes or suggests ways that group process could be facilitated. The structures which evaluate or measure the processes going on in a group include the "Group Function Review," the "Interim Objectives Assessment Scale," and the check lists about "How am I Doing" and the "Self-Discovery Test." These structures provide a way of feeding back information into the group on its own progress toward the group's defined goals. Other structures are designed to generate or facilitate processes, such as "The Moon Survival Problem," "Responsible Feedback," and the exercise which is perhaps the most controversial of all, the exercise on "Anonymous Feedback." The exercises generating group process, and particularly "Anonymous Feedback," should be used with caution, and then by trained facilitators.

A sixth cluster suggests structures for getting at feelings and attitudes of participants. Some of these require non-verbal modes of communicating feelings, which may be easier for participants not fluent in English but which may be more personal or intrusive for other participants. Examples of the non-verbal structures would include "Immediate Feelings," "Speaking Without Speaking," "Physical Communication," and "Role Playing Emotions." These are all more ambiguous and consequently less easy to control with regard to their outcome. The more analytical structures include "Cross-Culture Encounter," "We and You," Perceptual Set Exercise," and "Stereotypes." Other structures are suggested which will generate a range of attitudes and feelings for discussion by the group, such as "Lump Sum," "Dialogue Within Ourselves," and "The Most Memorable Experience of Your Childhood."

A seventh cluster of structures relates to community interaction, either through direct involvement in the community or through discussion of topics describing the community. The structures requiring direct involvement also require closer supervision, guidance and skillful debriefing to make the structure valuable for participants and less intrusive for members of the community. The direct involvement structures include "No Questions Asked," "The Cultural Treasure Hunt," the "Community Description Exercise," "Community Exposure," "Community Exploration," "Two Audio-Visual Approaches," and "Community Involvement." These all demonstrate how everyday experiences can be instructive and are perhaps more "structured" than they would first appear. It is also designed to sharpen participants' skills to observe evidence of their own cultural values around them. Other structures are designed to facilitate discussion of the community, such as "The American Studies Exercise" and "World Picture Test," which require less risk and direct involvement by participants.

The final two clusters of structures suggest ways in which a group leader can facilitate feedback to the group by participants, as through "Force Field

Analysis," "Points to Consider," or "Culturally Mixed Groups." These exercises might be appropriate when a group has slowed down for some unknown reason and the participants need to specify possible sources of resistance. The "Creative Problem Solving" technique is also potentially useful in either diagnosing a problem within the group or generating new data through group participation in a joint task.

Following the suggested structures, there is a list of other publications that include structures or exercises appropriate for use by intercultural groups. Any number of other handbooks not intended for intercultural groups are available for adaptation by small group facilitators. None of these exercises will provide a substitute for skilled leadership, but having specific exercises available increases the options open to a facilitator at any given point in the group. Sometimes just knowing that several useful structures are held in reserve puts a facilitator at ease, even when the exercises themselves are seldom employed. In other cases, the facilitator proceeding without structures gets into more trouble than would have resulted even from a badly prepared structured exercise. Thus, the choice is not between using or not using structures. The choice is between organizing planned or unplanned intercultural groups.

The field of intercultural communication desperately needs to guide organization of an intercultural group experience. In an attempt to contribute to such theory, we will speculate about possible arguments for and possible arguments against the use of structured exercises in intercultural group work.

Arguments for structures include the following:

1. There is research available that supports the appropriate use of exercises as resulting in favorable outcomes for intercultural groups.[1]
2. Structured exercises require less training and are able to extend the capability of intercultural group leaders who are just developing necessary group leadership skills.
3. Structured exercises can get a new group going more rapidly with less time required for warm-up when the group is meeting for a very limited period of time.
4. Structured exercises require less preparation time when they can be borrowed or applied from collections of already prepared materials.
5. Structured experiences define roles less ambiguously and may therefore be perceived as less threatening by persons from different cultures with more clearly stated expectations and more clearly

---

[1] See the bibliography in R. Brislin and P. Pedersen, *Cross-Cultural Orientation Programs*, New York, Gardner, 1976.

defined appropriate behavior.

6. A great deal of progress has been made on specific structured exercises to match a desired response, outcome, or change with a particular set of structured circumstances for groups or individuals.

7. Defining objectives is easier when the exercises are structured, and consequently, it is easier for participants to be articulate about the successful or unsuccessful results of the training.

8. Structured exercises, as they are more widely tested, contribute to a system of bringing about specific and desirable changes through intercultural conflict in ways that can be experimentally replicated and contribute to an intercultural theory.

9. Structuring an exercise forces both the facilitator and participants to be clear about their objectives, both individually and collectively as an intercultural group.

10. There is an abundance of structured exercises available in small group research and training designs that can be easily adapted to intercultural education.

Arguments against reliance upon structural exercises include the following points of view:

The structured exercise is culture-bound. American students are trained and experienced in role-taking and game-playing for educational purposes from kindergarten through college, and after, in vocational training. American facilitators unconsciously assume that visitors from other cultures have had equivalent experiences, which is usually not the case.

Some cultures use "pretend" situations extensively for serious purposes, but most do not. When a representative of a culture which separates game-playing from serious business like education is pressured into participation in a structured exercise, significant stresses result. Then the painful side-effects may become more intense. It is particularly difficult for a representative of a self-effacing culture like the Japanese to openly confront and oppose their group. The reaction of many Japanese students, for example, is to feel that it is not fair that they are forced into game playing, but because refusing to do so would be grossly impolite, they go along and suffer in silence.

A strong argument against structured exercises in intercultural group work is the unspoken assumption among Americans that openness contributes to understanding and has positive social value. Hiding your feelings and not revealing your thoughts has a much higher value in many cultures. Associated with the value of keeping thoughts and emotions private is the preference for indirection in interpersonal communication. An Easterner communicating appropriately seldom says what he means directly, but talks about the topic, relying upon the other person to intuit or guess his meaning. In this manner, two persons can explore a topic and open up new options, without commitment. To expect a person who has lived by indirection to "talk American" and "lay it on the line" is to place him in a state of tension that often generates a destructive emotional condition.

When we assume that openness is good, we violate a host of assumptions and values in other cultures that few facilitators think about. Americans assume that if we talk enough, the problem will be solved. Many cultures rely upon silence, and consider it more constructive and praiseworthy to refrain from speaking rather than to discuss the issue. When a person who *knows* that effective group work consists mainly of thinking together and picking up each other's thoughts through nonverbal cues is expected to talk his full share of time in a continuously verbal group, substantial psychic disarray is to be expected.

A byproduct of openness in structured exercises that has been too little discussed is the predicament of a person from a vertical society, one in which hierarchy and status are its main organizing elements. An individual from such a culture knows who he is and what he is expected to do by knowing who is above him in status, and who is inferior to him. Suddenly he finds himself in a structured exercise in which participants are divested of status. Everyone is assumed to be "as good as" everyone else, first names are used, and all talk to each other as equals. The vertical society person suffers a loss of identity. The only rules and procedures for talking with other human beings that he knows are arbitrarily abolished. When he is addressed inappropriately, he is shocked, and he finds himself unable to talk to others in his group in the specified open manner, for that would violate his life-long habits of politeness and civility. A facilitator might well try to understand the difficulties experienced by a person of some status in a vertical society who is expected to behave "like an American" in a structured exercise.

Many facilitators using structured exercises in groups of mixed cultures blandly take for granted that participants have superhuman abilities. For example, role playing the other person's culture, to be done profitably, would require many years of experience in and study of the other person's culture. As it is usually done, it is so superficial as to have little significance, and it is seldom if ever adequately debriefed. Further, many exercises assume that participants can explain their own behavior, and account for it. Most of the influences that shape the interpersonal interaction patterns of an individual are unknown to him, and the patterns themselves are largely out of awareness. If it takes a couple of years of psychoanalysis for a person to become slightly competent in describing his own normative behaviors, then the participant in an intercultural group should not be expected to reveal much valuable information about the ways in which his subculture conducts its interpersonal transactions.

A popular rationalization for using structured exercises is the assertion that those dealing with situational, mechanical sorts of behavior patterns, such as greetings, table manners, introducing one person to another, making requests or expressing gratitude are safe to use with all cultures because basic value orientations are not involved. Quite to the contrary, these seemingly superficial "sets of expectations" express and evolve from fundamental assumptions and values of a society. Thus, there is no such category as "casual" or "unimportant" behavior that differs from one culture to another. When any appropriate interaction activity is contrasted to that in another culture, the value systems they represent are in conflict. Perhaps exercises dealing in sets of expectations could be useful, if the objective is to gain understanding of the underlying value systems. But becoming familiar with mechanical differences in handling situations for their own sake may well cause more confusion than enlightenment.

The arguments above which challenge the use of structured exercises with intercultural groups are theoretical and deal with fundamental variables important to the mising of cultures. There are some more pitfalls that concern methodological problems contronting the facilitator. Perhaps the major hazard comes from availability and ease of use. Increasingly, the cumulative supply of structured exercises fosters a formula approach to the management of intercultural training. Instead of studying the particular persons in a group and devising ways to meet their unique needs, the temptation may well be to select from the wealth of available gimmicks the exercises that seem to fit the situation better than others. Ideally, the intercultural workshop or training program is a joint venture wherein facilitator and participants are free to modify plans and procedures as needs change and new needs are discovered. Structured exercises make this flexibility less likely.

Of course, the lazy or incompetent facilitator may be tempted to substitute structured exercises for skill. Actually, wringing maximum productivity out of a structured exercise requires the abilities of a highly skilled facilitator. The fact remains, however, that unskilled, inexperienced facilitators rely more on structured exercises than do their more talented and able colleagues.

We believe that a strong case can be made either for using or for not using structured exercises in intercultural groups. A collection of structures such as are provided in this publication, make available alternatives for stimulating and understanding the interaction of intercultural communication. The essential task will be to match favorable outcomes with those structures which, under certain conditions, facilitate progress. This collection of structures, used with discretion, provides a means for the intercultural group participant and leader to increase their learning and define favorable outcomes for themselves.

INTRODUCTION

The primary theme underlying this publication is that persons of any ethnic background and identification benefit from a multicultural development. The need for this development is entailed in the contemporary interweaving of cultures which importunes that people's survival skills transcend the challenges of their native society. In the state of Hawaii, for example, immigrants from Pacific Basin countries who do not develop social abilities required by American society subject themselves to a host of failure experiences that makes their adjustment to American ways difficult if not impossible. The members of the host culture bear an equal responsibility for adjusting their life styles to the degree necessary to comprehend and accommodate any unfamiliar behaviors of the immigrant and any cultural shifts the interaction generates.

Successfully adjusting to the many complex demands of an unfamiliar culture is a significant achievement. Peter S. Adler of Hawaii's East-West Center has penned an exciting description of the sort of individual who is socially and psychologically a product of twentieth century cultural interchange:

> "A new type of person whose orientation and view of the world profoundly transcends his indigenous culture is developing from the complex of social, political, economic, and educational interactions of our time... ...Multicultural man is the person who is intellectually and emotionally committed to the fundamental unity of all human beings while at the same time he recognizes, legitimizes, accepts and appreciates the fundamental differences that lie between people of different cultures."[1]

There are presently several systematic means by which information about foreign cultures can be imparted to those who seek such knowledge. Historical records, ethnographies, hologistic studies and most recently culture assimilators are some of those means. The field of human relations

1

training also provides a rich format by which culture learning may occur. This enduring field offers many techniques for teaching people about the various facets of human interaction. This is the subject of a book published by two of this volume's editors, Richard W. Brislin and Paul B. Pedersen, entitled *Cross-Cultural Orientation Programs* (John Wiley and Sons/Halsted Publishers). Among the several themes presented, this book describes comprehensively the forms and applications of available culture learning methodologies and the course of development of human relations training techniques in the area of cross-cultural understanding.

Techniques developed within the field of human relations training and which are described collectively as structured learning experiences provide the vehicle for culture learning in the present volume. Two of the most important phases in any cross-cultural training program are (1) selecting and utilizing structured experiences that reflect the learning needs of the participants and (2) adequately processing the data generated in the course of an exercise.

In regard to the first point, learning goals are best stated in behavioral terms and limited in their complexity and number so that they can be realistically met through an appropriate exercise.

Prior to an exercise, some time should be allotted to plan for the processing phase. It is often helpful to select one or more participants as observers and assessors of individual or total group performance in relation to the exercise objective. Then, following the exercise, the observer reports can be fed into the general processing dialogue. In this volume several exercises, such as "Process Observation: A Guide" and "The Fish Bowl," offer written formats to aid participant observers in their assessment of the group's work. But whether observers are used or not in the processing phase, extensive consideration should always be given to participants' immediate learning needs, the exercise objective, and how the present learning experiences connect with other program activities.

The person in charge of the structured experience is referred to in this volume as the facilitator. Generally, good facilitators closely monitor group processes and provide suggestions or leadership whenever processes deviate significantly from the acknowledged objectives of the group. They establish the groundrules and a congenial atmosphere which encourages group members to interact and acquire and exchange viewpoints reflective of the issues of concern to them. Facilitators can meet group needs best by refraining from participation when they perceive that the group's functioning is directly relevant to their learning needs.

Probably the two most vital tasks of the facilitator are to aid in selecting structured experiences that best meet the learning needs of participants and to see that adequate processing of data takes place following every exercise. Ideally, the facilitator should ensure that participants are aware of the implications of their experience, that they cognitively, affectively and behaviorally integrate particular knowledge, develop generalizations that apply to pertinent areas and involvements of their lives, and comprehend theoretical as well as concrete applications of their learning. Ideally too, the cross-cultural facilitator should personify the qualities Peter S. Adler attributed earlier in this writing to contemporary multicultural man.

In the structured experiences presented in this volume, emphasis is on values, feelings and attitudes, as well as on substantive knowledge, in regard to cross-cultural learning. Practical information is obviously necessary to acquire in order to effectively function in another culture. However, unless persons recognize their own culture-based values, feelings and attitudes, are able to communicate them to others, and experientially learn the logic of other cultural systems, practical information about another culture will be of little use.

Materials presented here were obtained from many sources and represented in their original form a variety of settings and purposes. However, in preparing the exercises for this publication, original settings and purposes were not emphasized. Rather, efforts were directed toward making structured experiences as adaptable as possible to cross-cultural objectives, such as enhancement of learning about one's own culture and about foreign cultures, and progress toward a multicultural identity.

Because the titles of many structured experiences are ambiguous and have limited value for identifying materials other than by their page number, the table of contents, therefore, categorizes the exercises according to their general objective in an effort to further identify them.

The editors hope that the readers will find this volume amenable to their purposes and will feel free to use and adapt the materials in whatever manner is desired to facilitate cross-cultural understanding.

[1] From "Beyond Cultural Identity: Reflections on Cultural and Multicultural Man," by Peter S. Adler in *Topics in Culture Learning,* Vol. 2, 1974. Richard W. Brislin, ed., East-West Center, Honolulu, Hawaii.

STRUCTURED CULTURE LEARNING EXPERIENCES

PARTICIPANT INTRODUCTION AND INITIAL GROUP EXPERIENCE

(1) INTRODUCING YOURSELF TO ANOTHER CULTURE

OBJECTIVE

To demonstrate different ways that a group can begin with a cultural emphasis by introducing the members to one another.

PARTICIPANTS

Three or more persons from different cultures. Facilitator.

MATERIALS

None.

SETTING

No special requirements.

TIME

Variable.

PROCEDURE

1) Each individual is asked to introduce himself or herself by means of a significant incident that happened to him or her demonstrating some aspect of his or her culture.

2) Each individual is asked to introduce himself or herself in his or her native language as he or she would introduce themselves back home and then provide a direct translation to English.

3) Each individual is asked to introduce themselves to the group nonverbally using any form they wish.

4) Each person is asked to name one important thing about themselves in addition to his or her name.

5) Each person is asked to introduce another member of the group from a different culture after a few minutes discussion with that person to get acquainted.

Designed by Robert Moran, University of Minnesota, 1973.

(2) MIXED CULTURE GROUPS

OBJECTIVE

To learn about values and behaviors common to people of other cultures and to develop awareness of the influence culture has on one's own values and behaviors.

PARTICIPANTS

Any size culturally mixed group. Facilitator.

MATERIALS

None required.

SETTING

Informal, at someone's home or a lounge with privacy. Natural seating arrangements without tables. Refreshments typical of the various cultures represented are recommended.

TIME

No limitation.

PROCEDURE

1) "My Home"
If participants are meeting together for the first time, one way of getting things started is to arrange people in a circle and ask them to write down the first five "un-guarded" words they can think of when the name of their country (or perhaps home town) is mentioned. The facilitator then asks them to read off their lists and explain why they chose particular words. This exercise can then be repeated, using as a focus instead the town where the group is presently gathered. The purpose of the second step is to indicate various perceptions of a similar community and possible cultural differences at the same time.

2) Introducing Ourselves
As a second step, each participant is asked to pair off with someone whom he doesn't know. The leader asks each one to get to know the other for the purpose of introducing him to the rest of the group. The tone of the session should be relaxed and the leader should encourage friendly laughter--the goal being something more than a casual conversation, yet something different from a formal class in cultural anthropology.

3) My Favorite Pastimes[1]
As group members become better acquainted, another useful exercise can be used, which helps the participants get acquainted with the different values practiced by others in the group. They are asked to list on a piece of paper the ten (or twenty) things they like best to do.

Once this is done, they are asked to write a "p" next to each item which requires other people, and an "m" beside each item which requires more than a small amount of money to do. Finally, they are asked to go back over their lists and make a note of how long it has been since last they did the particular activity. A sharing and discussion of the lists in smaller groups will bring out values as reflected by practices of the various societies involved. The leader can help by suggesting that each member tell his colleagues the extent to which other people in his society might agree with the list he drew up and what their lists might contain and why.

The leader should encourage participants to identify basic differences and similarities revealed by the exercise, in the ways people choose to spend their time. As before, however, he should keep his own partici- pation to a minimum, trying instead to have the members explain their conclusions to each other.

4) Social Customs
   With the leader doing little more than offering the topics, members are asked to work in groups of three, explaining to each other about their own personal experiences with regard to how children are raised in their societies, whom children respect the most, how people become engaged and marry, or how local economic life is carried out. After the discus- sions, the members come together again and the leader asks for volun- teers to report back to the full group what they have learned from the others. A skillful group leader is necessary to bring out key points and contrasts, temper idealized interpretations of societies, or occa- sionally calm potentially disruptive arguments by participants from rival countries.

[1]Sidney Simon, Workshop in Value Clarification (unpublished outline). Amherst, Massachusetts: The University of Massachusetts. Winter, 1970.

This exercise was adapted from "Mixed Culture Groups," in A Manual of Teaching Techniques for Intercultural Education (UNESCO), October, 1971. Henry Holmes and Stephen Guild, eds.

(3)   TELLING ABOUT THE GROUP AFTERWARD

OBJECTIVE

To assist members of a group in stating their goals and objectives during the first meeting or early in the group when members are attempting to define or describe their expectations for the group experience.

PARTICIPANTS

Any size group divided into dyads.   Facilitator.

MATERIALS

None.

SETTING

No special requirements.

TIME

Unlimited.

PROCEDURE

1) Ask each member to select one other person and divide up in dyads.

2) Each member will carry on a conversation with his or her partner about what happened in the group, as though this were the next day and the group was already over.

3) Each member will have an opportunity to rehearse telling others about the group experience as if it were already over.

4) Each member will help others in discussion identify those goals which appeared most frequently.

5) If possible it would be ideal to have persons from the same culture in each dyad. This would allow participants to rehearse telling about the group to their own back-home referent culture group.

Developed by Paul Pedersen, University of Minnesota.

DYNAMICS OF COMMUNICATION

(4) FOLLOWING DIRECTIONS

OBJECTIVE

To clarify for participants the formats of their communication and the difficulties and inaccuracies encountered when implementing those formats.

PARTICIPANTS

Any number of dyads, each individual in a given dyad representing a different culture. Facilitator.

MATERIALS

1) One or more index cards for each participant (see example).
2) Answer sheets and pencils for each participant.

SETTING

Dyads should be seated around a table. If there are several dyads, each should be seated at a different table.

TIME

Variable, depending on participant characteristics, number of cards per participant, and processing phase; anywhere from ten minutes to an hour or more.

PROCEDURE

1) Participants are divided into culturally mixed dyads and seated around tables.

2) At each table, one participant sits on one side of the table and is designated as "source", the other is seated on the other side and is designated as "respondent".

3) Each participant is given an answer sheet and one or more index cards. The answer sheets as shown in the example contain eight matrices of twenty-five dots each. The cards contain one matrix of twenty-five dots, on which five of the dots are connected by five lines. Each card design is unique.

4) Each source must verbally communicate the design on one of his cards to the respondent seated across from him who must reproduce it on one of the blank matrices on his answer sheet within a recommended time limit of ten to fifteen seconds.

5) Participants alternate being sources and respondents and may change their partners with each new round of activity.

6) Facilitator leads discussion tying in participants' experience with the exercise objective, emphasizing the role cultural difference may play in confounding communication.

7) Suggested variations of this exercise are:

A. Ask participants to draw their own designs and then communicate them to each other.

B. Draw and communicate more complex designs (eight dots and eight lines) in the same amount of time.

C. Communicate designs drawn on irregular matrices.

D. If several dyads take part in the exercise, make each correct communication worth one point. Besides the element of inter-dyad competition, the success of each dyad member becomes contingent upon the success of the other. Some interesting affective data may be generated for discussion.

Following Directions   Answer Sheet

1. o   o   o   o   o   2. o   o   o   o   o

    o   o   o   o   o   o   o   o   o   o

    o   o   o   o   o   o   o   o   o   o

    o   o   o   o   o   o   o   o   o   o

    o   o   o   o   o   o   o   o   o   o

3. o   o   o   o   o   4. o   o   o   o   o

    o   o   o   o   o   o   o   o   o   o

    o   o   o   o   o   o   o   o   o   o

    o   o   o   o   o   o   o   o   o   o

    o   o   o   o   o   o   o   o   o   o

5. o   o   o   o   o   6. o   o   o   o   o

    o   o   o   o   o   o   o   o   o   o

    o   o   o   o   o   o   o   o   o   o

    o   o   o   o   o   o   o   o   o   o

    o   o   o   o   o   o   o   o   o   o

7. o   o   o   o   o   8. o   o   o   o   o

    o   o   o   o   o   o   o   o   o   o

    o   o   o   o   o   o   o   o   o   o

    o   o   o   o   o   o   o   o   o   o

    o   o   o   o   o   o   o   o   o   o

INDEX CARD

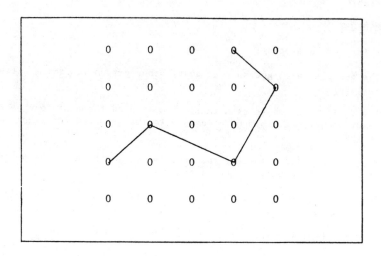

Contributed by Royal Freuhling, University of Hawaii, 1975.

---

(5) RUMOR TRANSMISSION USING MULTIPLE TRANSLATIONS

OBJECTIVE

To demonstrate the difficulty of translating meaning accurately to another language.

PARTICIPANTS

Three or more persons who speak different languages. Facilitator.

MATERIALS

None.

SETTING

No special requirements.

TIME

Variable.

PROCEDURE

1) Early in a group meeting:

A. The group is arranged so that every other person is from a different culture.

B. The facilitator whispers a fairly complicated three or four sentence rumor about some topic of relevance to the group to the first person in the circle.

C. Each member will translate the rumor and pass it on to the person sitting next to him in a new language.

D. The final person will translate the rumor into English and tell it to the group.

E. Discuss the experience in regard to the exercise objective.

Designed by Paul Pedersen, University of Minnesota.

---

(6) INTERCULTURAL COMMUNICATION WORKSHOP EXERCISE

OBJECTIVE

To enable participants to hear their discussion and interaction.

PARTICIPANTS

Three or more persons from various cultures. Facilitator.

MATERIALS

Tape recorder.

SETTING

No special requirements.

TIME

Approximately two hours.

PROCEDURE

1) At the beginning of the meeting, the facilitator turns on the recorder and the meeting proceeds as usual.

2) After forty-five minutes, the facilitator stops the recorder and the discussion and tells the group the task for the rest of the meeting pertains to the recorded discussion.

3) Participants are told they can merely listen to the recording or they can stop the tape at any time and discuss it.

4) Suggested discussion inputs that can be related to cross-cultural themes are given by the facilitator:

- what did you mean when you said that? I didn't ask then but I'd like to now . . . .
- I was feeling angry when you were talking . . . .
- You didn't say anything - were you bored . . . .

Designed by Robert Moran, University of Minnesota.

---

(7) CROSS-CULTURAL TRADE-OFF

OBJECTIVE

To improve the communication and relationship between participants.

PARTICIPANTS

Designed for two persons of different cultural backgrounds who know one another but can be modified for three or more persons.

MATERIALS

Paper and pencils.

SETTING

No special requirements.

<u>TIME</u>

Each step should entail about one hour's time.

<u>PROCEDURE</u>

STEP 1.

(1) Participants must agree on a time and place to do the game togethe

(2) Participants must want to cooperate.

(3) Participants must agree to respect confidences entrusted to them by the other partner.

(4) Participants must be open to the cultural and cross-cultural bases and dimensions of each experience they undergo.

STEP 2.

Participants make a list, being as specific as possible, of:

1. "Things you do or say which make me feel good."
2. "Things you do or say which make me feel bad."
3. "Things I do toward you which make me feel good."
4. "Things I do which I regret or make me feel bad."

Participants then exchange papers, read what they have written, and discuss the feelings they share.

STEP 3.

Participants respond to a series of adjectives by placing a check ($\checkmark$) besides these adjectives BEST describing themselves in the first two columns and their partner in the last two columns.

Also, an 'X' should be placed beside these adjectives that LEAST descri themselves and their partner. Participants may write in any specific comments that would help them understand each other's reaction.

ADJECTIVE	Me As I See Myself	Me As I Want To Be	You As I See You	You As I Want You To Be	COMME
1. adventurous					
2. false					
3. affectionate					
4. ambitious					
5. anxious for approval					
6. appreciative					
7. argumentative					
8. big-hearted					
9. neat					

ADJECTIVE	Me As I See Myself	Me As I Want To Be	You As I See You	You As I Want You To Be	COMMENTS
10. competitive					
11. complaining					
12. critical of others					
13. demanding					
14. distant					
15. dogmatic					
16. dominating					
17. easily angered					
18. easily discouraged					
19. easily influenced					
20. efficient					
21. encouraging					
22. enthusiastic					
23. forgiving					
24. frank, forthright					
25. fun-loving					
26. give praise readily					
27. good listener					
28. helpful					
29. indifferent to others					
30. impulsive					
31. intolerant					
32. jealous					
33. kind					
34. optimistic					
35. loud					
36. independent					
37. orderly					
38. needs much praise					
39. obedient					
40. rebellious					
41. resentful					
42. responsible					
43. sarcastic					
44. discourteous					
45. self-centered					
46. self-respecting					
47. self-satisfied					
48. sentimental					
49. show love					
50. shrewd, devious					
51. shy					
52. sociable					
53. stern					
54. submissive					
55. successful					
56. sympathetic					
57. tactful					
58. talkative					
59. teasing					

ADJECTIVE	Me As I See Myself	Me As I Want To Be	You As I See You	You As I Want You To Be	COMMEN
60. thorough					
61. thoughtful					
62. touchy, can't be kidded					
63. trusting					
64. uncommunicative					
65. understanding					
66. varied interests					
67. very dependent on others					
68. well-mannered					
69. willing worker					

STEP 4.

Partners compare:

1. Your view of yourself and your partner's view of you.
2. Your ideal for yourself and your partner's ideal for himself or herself.
3. Your real view of yourself and your ideal for yourself.

Discuss the way you view yourself and the aspirations or goals you have with your partner. Are you being fair to yourself? Are you being fair to your partner?

STEP 5.

This step has two moves:

1. The first move builds on the positive shared feelings and on things you and I have in common. This may set guidelines for conduct we both want to continue and a basis for the future.

2. The second move focuses on difference, disagreement and conflict between you and me.   In this move we can seek to clarify the difficulty and find ways to work together.

Fill in the blanks below:

"Differences and
disagreements
between you and me are...

"The source of our
disagreement seems
to be . . .

"I handle these
disagreements by . . .

"You handle the
disagreements by . . .

"I might try . . .

"You might try . . .

"I think this
way might work
because . . .

STEP 6.

Participants write about some personal problem that their partner may
help them solve according to the following format:

Situation,
problem or
difference
_____

What I intend
to do about it.
_____

What I might
do in spite
of myself
_____

How I would like
you to help me
_____

STEP 7.

Review previous steps and findings. The whole idea of this exercise
is to help participants learn from each other, share their feelings
and reactions, views and ideals, areas of agreement and disagreement.
Hopefully cross-cultural relationships will work better now than
before the game was undertaken.

Adapted from Cross-Cultural Trade-Off, by Paul Pedersen.

CLARIFICATION OF VALUES

(8) CRITICAL INCIDENTS

OBJECTIVE

To provide experience analyzing critical cultural incidents and attempting to reach a judgment consensus with a group regarding the incident.

PARTICIPANTS

Three or more persons. Facilitator.

MATERIALS

Ten to twenty critical incidents, answer sheets, pencils.

SETTING

No special requirements.

TIME

Variable; at least thirty to forty-five minutes.

PROCEDURE

1) Each critical incident is a short (ten to twenty lines) account of a cultural event, whose outcome has cross-cultural significance (see example). Facilitators are encouraged to develop incidents from their own experience. Several of these incidents are presented to participants, along with an answer sheet.

2) The answer sheet is a "forced choice" technique whereby participants must make a judgment on the action which the incident describes. The sheet gives a scale of "Completely agree" (1) to "Completely disagree" (9) for each action described, and space for a brief justification of the rating. The facilitator emphasizes that there are no "right" answers to any of the incidents.

3) Each participant responds individually on paper to each incident. Then all are brought together in groups of four or five, and asked to:

a. Arrive at a group <u>consensus</u> rating;
b. Give a mutually agreeable <u>reason</u> for the rating, and
c. An acceptable substitute action in the incident.

(Voting or averaging is not allowed; a true consensus is the aim.)

Adapted from "Critical Incidents" in <u>A Manual of Teaching Techniques for Intercultural Education</u>, (UNESCO), October, 1971. Henry Holmes and Stephen Guild, eds.

CRITICAL INCIDENTS EXERCISE

For each incident, select your reaction from the following scale, then answer the other questions. The number you select should indicate the extent to which you agree with the opinions, attitudes, or actions of the person described in each incident.

1. Completely disagree
2. Almost completely disagree
3. Disagree quite a bit
4. Disagree more than agree
5. Neutral
6. Agree more than disagree
7. Agree quite a bit
8. Almost completely agree
9. Completely agree

1. Rating _____ What would you do?
   Why?

2. Rating _____ What would you do?
   Why?

3. Rating _____ What would you do?
   Why?

4. Rating _____ What would you do?
   Why?

5. Rating _____ What would you do?
   Why?

6. Rating _____ What would you do?
   Why?

7. Rating _____ What would you do?
   Why?

8. Rating _____ What would you do?
   Why?

9. Rating _____ What would you do?
   Why?

10. Rating _____ What would you do?
    Why?

A CRITICAL INCIDENT

An American in Viet Nam recalls an illuminating story told him by a Vietnamese who complained about a lack of understanding between the two allies. They were discussing the fate of a province chief named Vong, once hailed by the Americans as the best province chief in Vietnam. Vong was accused of embezzling some 300,000 American dollars earmarked for an airstrip, and was tried and sentenced to be executed. It seemed a harsh sentence, considering the corruption prevalent at the time, and the American asked the Vietnamese if he agreed.

"No," the Vietnamese said, "Vong should be executed because he's a stupid man."

"Stupid? Because he got caught?" the American asked.

The Vietnamese impatiently shook his head. "No, no, not because he took the money," he said. "That is not important. But you know what this stupid man did? He pacified six more hamlets than his quota. This caused the general who gave him the quota to lose face, and that is stupid."

The perplexed American said, "In America, he'd get a medal for exceeding his quota." The Vietnamese shook his head and said, "You Americans will never understand the Vietnamese."

What aspects of the incident are significant in describing the difference in opinion between these two persons?

---

(9) CASE STUDIES

OBJECTIVE

To generate appreciation of important cultural problems and provide experience diagnosing and resolving conflicts of values, attitudes, or feelings.

PARTICIPANTS

Three or more persons. Facilitator.

MATERIALS

Several case studies organized around a similar theme, pencils.

SETTING

No special requirements.

TIME

Variable; at least thirty to forty-five minutes.

PROCEDURE

1) Participants read the case and write a paragraph of analysis and recommendation for action.

2) The facilitator then introduces questions about the case for discussion.

3) Finally, the facilitator asks particiapnts to write a new analysis of the case, which may be shared among the members of the group.

Case Study and Discussion Guide: Example from Malaysia

The frail, old, almost totally blind lady appeared at every clinic session and sat on the dirt floor enjoying the activity. She was dirty and dishevelled, and obviously had very little, even by Malaysian Kampong (local village) standards.

One day the visiting nurse happened upon this woman in her kampong. She lived by herself in a rundown shack about 10 by 10 feet. When questioned how she obtained her food, she said she was often hungry, as she only received food when she worked for others--pounding rice, looking after the children, and the like.

The nurse sought to obtain help for the woman. It was finally resolved that she would receive a small pension from the Department of Welfare which would be ample for her needs.

At each weekly clinic, the woman continued to appear. She had become a center of attention, laughed and joked freely, and obviously enjoyed her increased prestige. No change was noted in her physical status, however. She continued to wear the same dirty black dress and looked no better fed.

The nurse asked one of the rural health nurses to find out if the woman needed help in getting to a shop to buy the goods she seemed so sorely in need of.

In squatting near the woman, the rural health nurse noted a wad of bills in the woman's basket. "Wah," she said, "It is all here. You have spent nothing. Why is that?"

The woman laughed and then explained: "I am saving it all for my funeral."

Discussion Guide:

How do people approach activity?

What are the important goals in life?

What is the nature of humour?

What is the nature of social reciprocity?

What is the attitude toward problem solving?

What is the nature of property?

What are the relationships between man and nature?

What personal qualities are valued?

What are the attitudes toward change?

Adapted from "Case Studies" in A Manual of Teaching Techniques for Inter-cultural Education (UNESCO). October, 1971. Henry Holmes and Stephen Guild, eds.

---

(10) THE PARABLE

OBJECTIVE

To clarify cultural differences and similarities among members of a group by stimulating awareness of problems in transmitting one's own ideas and listening to others. and by demonstrating how decisions are determined by cultural values.

PARTICIPANTS

At least eight persons of diverse cultural backgrounds. Facilitator.

MATERIALS

Chalkboard and chalk, paper and pencils.

SETTING

Seating arrangement allowing chairs to be moved into small groups.

TIME

At least thirty minutes.

PROCEDURE

1) The leader tells the following parable to the group, illustrating with rough chalkboard drawings if he chooses:

"Rosemary is a girl of about 21 years of age. For several months she has been engaged to a young man named -- let's call him Geoffrey. The problem she faces is that between her and her betrothed there lies a river. No ordinary river mind you, but a deep, wide river infested with hungry crocodiles.

"Rosemary ponders how she can cross the river. She thinks of a man she knows who has a boat. We'll call him Sinbad. So she approaches Sinbad, asking him to take her across. He replies, 'Yes, I'll take you across if you'll spend the night with me.' Shocked at this offer, she turns to another acquaintance, a certain Frederick, and tells him her story. Fredrick responds by saying, 'Yes, Rosemary, I understand your problem -- but -- it's your problem, not mine.' Rosemary decides to return to Sinbad, spends the night with him, and in the morning he takes her across the river.

"Her reunion with Geoffrey is warm. But on the evening before they are to be married, Rosemary feels compelled to tell Geoffrey how she succeeded in getting across the river. Geoffrey responds by saying, 'I wouldn't marry you if you were the last woman on earth.'

"Finally, at her wits' end, Rosemary turns to our last character, Dennis. Dennis listens to her story and says, 'Well, Rosemary, I don't love you . . . . but I will marry you.' And that's all we know of the story."

2) The facilitator asks each participant to write down on a piece of paper, in rank order, the characters whose behavior he most approves, plus a sentence or two explaining his first choice.

3) Next, participants are split into groups of four or five and asked to share -- each with the others in his group -- the choices he made. Not more than ten to fifteen minutes should be allowed for this discussion; its main purpose is to raise the issues, not to exhaust them.

4) He asks, "Would anyone care to volunteer anything you learned as a result of the discussion you have just had -- anything at all?" He should allow a short discussion to follow and call for a few other volunteers to share what they have learned.

5) He may then ask the group, "Can anyone point to some place, some source within your own past where you learned the values that caused you to take the position that you did?" Participants will probably have some difficulty with this question; no matter. It is intended to be a difficult question.

6) Next the facilitator says, "Now I would like you to ask yourselves - I don't want an answer on this one, just want you to consider -- how many of you feel you could faithfully re-state, to the satisfaction of some-one else in your small group, the point of view, the <u>Value</u> being express-ed by that person? Again, I don't want you to answer, just think about the question."

7) The leader may then summarize the session briefly, making the following points:

    a. Values come out of one's cultural background. They are difficult to track down to a particular source and are often part of a person's unconscious behavior.

    b. Within any particular culture a person's values are usually very logical. They make sense in that culture.

    c. For these reasons people should be very cautious about making moral judgment about other people's values.

    d. If one really wants to understand someone else, one has to listen extremely well and really try to "get inside" the other person. This is the reason for the question, "How accurately do you think you could re-state someone else's opinion?" Those of you who would have to answer "not very" have some work to do.

    e. What are some other areas in life where people's values differ?

    f. Now that you are acquainted with some people from other cultures, you may want to investigate, directly with them, some of the values and beliefs which they prize the most.

8) The leader should conclude the session almost as if it were the beginning, rather than the end, of a learning experience. One way to do this is simply to say that this is the end of the formal session and then join one of the small groups for conversation, rather than leave the room.

"The Parable" was contributed in its original form by Sidney Simon, Professor of Education, University of Massachusetts, to <u>A Manual of Teaching Techniques for Intercultural Education</u> (UNESCO). October, 1971. Henry Holmes and Stephen Guild, eds.

(11) LETTERS TO THE EDITOR

OBJECTIVE

To reveal standards of behavior and values typical of various cultures.

PARTICIPANTS

At least two groups of three persons each, each person representing a different culture. Facilitator.

MATERIALS

"Letters to the Editor" drawn from actual newspapers or simulated "Letters." Paper and pencils.

SETTING

No special requirements.

TIME

Variable; at least one hour.

PROCEDURE

1) "Letters to the Editor" (real or simulated) are given to each participant to examine. The participant then writes a ten-minute reply to the
letter.

2) Mixed culture groups of three are formed to share opinions and develop
a joint reply which "their" newspaper will print and release to the
larger group.

3) The facilitator asks participants to express to the larger group any
points of view they feel they gained during small group discussions
with persons of other cultures and viewpoints.

4) Suggested options are: To ask participants to prepare replies as if they
were members of cultures other than their own; participants might write
letters of their own and exchange them with other participants who then
provide replies · An option for the facilitator at the end is to read
actual replies printed by the newspaper and invite reactions from participants.

Adapted from "Letters to the Editor" in A Manual of Teaching Techniques for
Intercultural Education (UNESCO). October, 1971. Henry Holmes and Stephen
Guild, eds.

(12) CROSS-CULTURAL TRAINING EXERCISE FOR INTERPRETING POLICY

OBJECTIVE

To determine culture-specific patterns of common and variant interpretations, as well as level of comprehension of written material containing word deletions.

PARTICIPANTS

Three or more persons. Facilitator.

MATERIALS

Pencils.

SETTING

No special requirements.

TIME

At least twenty minutes to one-half hour (unlimited).

PROCEDURE

1) The facilitator selects one or more paragraphs drawn from institutional rhetoric involving cross-cultural values.

2) The facilitator then omits at least ten or fifteen words, keeping the space where these words were extracted blank for the participants to write in his own word as he considers appropriate.

3) Each participant is given a copy of the paragraph and a pencil.

4) Then, after filling in the blanks to give the paragraph meaning, the group compares their interpretations and discusses them according to culture-specific variables.

Example:*

"The Board of Regents has _____ itself and the University of Minnesota to the policy that there shall be no _____ in the treat- ment of _____ because of _____. This is a guiding policy in the _____ of students in all colleges and in their _____. It is also to be a governing principle in University-owned and University-approved housing, in food services, student unions, extra-curricular activities and all other student and staff services. This policy must also be _____ in the _____ of students either by the University or by _____ through the University and in the

_____ of faculty and civil service staff."

*Statement on Human Rights, University of Minnesota 71-72 Bulletin on General Information.

Designed by Paul Pedersen, University of Minnesota.

---

(13) A FREE DRAWING TEST TO DEMONSTRATE CROSS-CULTURAL DIFFERENCES

OBJECTIVE

To produce data on differential subconscious responses to culture-loaded concepts.

PARTICIPANTS

Culturally diversified group of moderate size. Facilitator.

MATERIALS

Pencils and several blank sheets of paper for each participant.

SETTING

Chairs and drawing surfaces for each participant. Privacy during drawing sessions is recommended.

TIME

Time limit is optional.

PROCEDURE

1) Select a number of concepts (nouns, verbs, etc.) that seem to the group members to be clearly related to their respective cultures.

2) Ask each member to draw an "X" in the middle of a blank sheet of paper.

3) Ask each member to place his pencil on the center of the "X" and begin drawing when the facilitator mentions one of the previously selected concepts. The members should not be given any guidance on what to draw but merely instructed to form one continuous line in any direction or shape as they are motivated by the announced concept.

4) Apply a scoring technique to compare the drawings, looking at the data according to whether the drawing is open, closed, large, small, complex, simple, requiring more time, requiring less time, angular, rounded, number of directional changes, number of reversals, recognizable picture, begins with an up-stroke, begins with down-stroke, ends with an up-stroke, ends with a down-stroke, etc. Other criteria to compare the drawings may be suggested by the group, growing out of apparent similarities and differences.

5) Discuss whether similarities and differences in the drawings seem to coincide with cultural differences in the group in terms of the covert effects culture has on behavior.

---

(14) COMPARING PEOPLE TO OBJECTS

OBJECTIVE

To help the group clarify cultural differences which seem to be affecting the group's performance.

PARTICIPANTS

Three or more persons from different cultures. Facilitator.

MATERIALS

None.

SETTING

No special requirements.

TIME

Variable.

PROCEDURE

1) The facilitator instructs each member to look around the room and find one object that is like them in some way, representing if possible one or more cultural values of their background.

2) The facilitator may model this difficult task by selecting an object himself (like a piece of chalk that is hard and brittle and gives of itself until it is finally used up completely) and describing how he is like that object.

3) The members will each in turn describe how they are like one or another object in the room.

4) Members may then discuss the cultural differences which emerge.

Designed by Paul Pedersen, University of Minnesota.

---

(15) VALUE STATEMENTS EXERCISE

OBJECTIVE

Clarification of values that typify persons from different cultures.

PARTICIPANTS

One or more persons. Facilitator if done as a group exercise. Group members should represent a variety of cultures.

MATERIALS

Pencils.

SETTING

No special requirements.

TIME

At least ten to fifteen minutes.

PROCEDURE

1) Each participant should have a copy of the exercise statements and indicate individually whether they agree or disagree with each of the statements.

2) If done as a group exercise, responses should be compared and discussed.

1. It is the man who stands alone who excites our admiration.

2. The individualist is the man who is most likely to discover the best road to a new future.

3. In most groups it is better to choose somebody to take charge and run

things, and then hold him responsible, even if he does some things the members do not like.

4. The most rewarding object of study any man can find is his own inner life.

5. There should be equality for everyone--because we are all human beings.

6. Good group members should accept criticisms of their points of view without argument, in order to preserve a harmonious group.

7. Not to attain happiness, but to be worthy of it, is the purpose of our existence.

8. Man's future depends primarily upon what he does, not upon what he feels or what he thinks.

9. He has achieved success who has lived well, laughed often, and loved much.

10. A well-raised child is one who does not have to be told twice to do something.

11. The facts on crime and sexual immorality show that we will have to crack down harder on young people if we are going to save our moral standards.

12. There has been too much talk and not enough real action in doing away with racial discrimination.

13. Heaven and hell are products of man's imagination and do not actually exist.

14. Let us eat, drink, and be merry, for tomorrow we die.

15. A rich life requires constant activity, the use of muscles, and openness to adventure.

16. A teen-ager should be allowed to decide most things for himself.

17. Character and honesty will tell in the long run; most people get pretty much what they deserve.

18. The most important function of modern leaders is to bring about the accomplishment of practical goals.

19. In life an individual should for the most part "go it alone," assuring himself of privacy, having much time to himself, attempting to control his own life.

20. Human nature being what it is, there will always be war and conflict.

21. Friendship should go just so far in working relationships.

22. What youth needs most is strict discipline, rugged determination, and the will to work and fight for family and country.

23. There should be a definite hierarchy in an organization, with definite duties for everybody.

24. No time is better spent than that devoted to thinking about the ultimate purposes of life.

25. Depressions are like occasional headaches and stomach aches, it is natural for even the healthiest society to have them once in a while.

26. In any group, it is more important to keep a friendly atmosphere than to be efficient.

27. A man must make his own decisions, uninfluenced by the opinions of others.

28. Obedience and respect for authority are the most important virtues children should learn.

29. In choosing a husband, a woman will do well to put ambition at the top of her list of desirable qualities.

30. In a small group there should be no real leaders--everybody should have an equal say.

31. To lay down your life for a friend--this is the summit of a good life.

32. You have to respect authority and when you stop respecting authority, your situation is not worth much.

33. Man should control his bodily senses, his emotions, feelings, and wishes.

34. When a person has a problem or worry, it is best for him not to think about it, but to keep busy with more cheerful things.

35. We are all born to love--it is the principle of existence and its only true end.

36. When we live in the proper way--stay in harmony with the forces of nature and keep all that we have in good condition, then all will go along well in the world.

37. A good group is democratic--the members should talk things over and decide unanimously what should be done.

38. Every person should have complete faith in some supernatural power whose decisions he obeys without question.

39. The past is dead, there are new worlds to conquer, the world belongs to the future.

40. The most important qualities of a real man are determination and driving ambition.

41. The greatest satisfaction in life is a feeling of the actuality of the present, of tireless activity, movement, and doing.

42. No matter what the circumstances, one should never arbitrarily tell people what they have to do.

43. The most important aim of the churches at the present time should be to encourage spiritual worship and a sense of communion with the highest.

---

(16) IMPLICIT ASSUMPTIONS CHECKLIST EXERCISE

OBJECTIVE

To identify American values, as well as Contrast-American values, that determine conflicting points of view in a cross-cultural encounter.

PARTICIPANTS

One or more persons. If done as a group exercise a facilitator should be present and group members should represent several cultures.

MATERIALS

Paper and pencils or blackboard and chalk are desirable though not essential.

SETTING

No special requirements.

TIME

Variable.

PROCEDURE

1) Identify a specific conflict situation of your own experience between two persons from different cultural backgrounds.

2) Check those values and behaviors which distinguish the persons who were involved in that situation against the information provided in Table I.

3) If several persons participated in the exercise, discuss with the others your conclusions about how those values may be understood, modified or directed to reconcile the conflict toward greater harmony and productivity.

Table 1

SUMMARY OF CULTURAL ASSUMPTIONS AND VALUES*

American	Contrast-American

1. Definition of Activity
   a. How do people approach activity?
      1) concern with "doing", progress, change--------------------------------- "being"
         external achievement------------------ spontaneous expressions
      2) optimistic, striving------------------ fatalistic

   b. What is the desirable pace of life?
      1) fast, busy---------------------------- steady, rhythmic
      2) driving------------------------------- noncompulsive

   c. How important are goals in planning?
      1) stress means, procedures, techniques--- stress final goals

   d. What are important goals in life?
      1) material goals------------------------ spiritual goals
      2) comfort and absence of pain----------- fullness of pleasure and pain
      3) activity------------------------------ experience

   e. Where does responsibility for decisions lie?
      1) responsibility lies with each individual----------------------------- function of a group or resides in a role (dual contrast)

   f. At what level do people live?
      1) operational, goals evaluated in terms of consequence--------------------- experimental truth

   g. On what basis do people evaluate?
      1) utility (does it work?)--------------- essence (ideal)

   h. Who should make decisions?
      1) the people affected------------------- those with proper authority

   i. What is the nature of problem-solving?
      1) planning behavior--------------------- coping behavior

American	Contrast-American

2) anticipates consequences------------ classifies the situation

j. What is the nature of learning?
   1) learner is active (student-centered
      learning)-------------------------- learner is passive (aerial rote learning)

2. Definition of Social Relations
   a. How are roles defined?
      attained--------------------------------- ascribed
      loosely---------------------------------- tightly
      generally-------------------------------- specifically

   b. How do people relate to others whose status
      is different?
      1) stress equality----------------------- stress hierarchical ranks
         minimize differences------------------- stress differences, especially to superiors
      2) stress informality and spontaneity----- stress formality, behavior more easily anticipated

   c. How are sex roles defined?
      similar, overlapping--------------------- distinct
      sex equality----------------------------- male superiority
      friends of both sexes-------------------- friends of same sex only
      less legitimized------------------------- legitimized

   d. What are members' rights and duties in a group?
      1) assumes limited liability------------- assumes unlimited liability
      2) joins group to seek own goals---------- accepts constraint by group
      3) active members can influence group----- leader runs group, members do not

   e. How do people judge others?
      1) specific abilities or interests-------- overall individuality of person and his status
      2) task-centered-------------------------- person-centered
      3) fragmentary involvement---------------- total involvement

   f. What is the meaning of friendship?
      1) social friendship--------------------- intense friendship
         (short commitment, friends shared)   (long commitment, friends are exclusive)

	American	Contrast-American

g. What is the nature of social reciprocity?
  1) real only-------------------------------- ideal and real
  2) nonbinding (Dutch treat)--------------- binding
  3) equal (Dutch treat)-------------------- unequal

h. How do people regard friendly aggression in
   social interaction?
  1) acceptable, interesting, fun----------- not acceptable, embar-
                                             rassing

3. Motivation
   a. What is motivating force?
     1) achievement--------------------------- ascription

   b. How is person-person competition evaluated?
     1) as constructive, healthy-------------- as destructive, anti-
                                              social

4. Perception of the World (World View)
   a. What is the (natural) world like?
     1) physical----------------------------- spiritual
     2) mechanical--------------------------- organic
     3) use of machines---------------------- disuse of machines

   b. How does the world operate?
     1) in a rational, learnable, controllable
        manner------------------------------- in a mystically ordered,
                                             spiritually conceivable
                                             manner (fate, divination)
     2) chance and probability--------------- no chance or probability

   c. What is the nature of man?
     1) apart from nature or from any
        hierarchy---------------------------- part of nature or of
                                             some hierarchy (dual
                                             contrast)
     2) impermanent, not fixed, changeable----- permanent, fixed, not
                                             changeable

   d. What are the relationships between man and
      nature?
     1) good is unlimited--------------------- good is limited
     2) man should modify nature for his ends-- man should accept the
                                             natural order
     3) good health and material comforts ex-
        pected and desired------------------- some disease and materi-
                                             al misery are natural,
                                             to be expected

American	Contrast-American

e. What is the nature of truth? goodness?
    1) tentative (working type)--------------- definite
    2) relative to circumstances-------------- absolute
    3) experience analyzed in separate com-
        ponents dichotomies------------------ experience appre-
                                    hended as a
                                    whole

f. How is time defined? Valued?
    1) future (anticipated)------------------- past (remembrance) or
                                    present experience
                                    (dual contrast)
    2) precise units------------------------- undifferentiated
    3) limited resource--------------------- not limited (not resource)
    4) lineal------------------------------- circular, undifferentiate

g. What is the nature of property?
    1) private ownership important as exten-
        sion of self----------------------- use for "natural" purpose
                                    regardless of ownership

5. Perception of the Self and the Individual
  a. In what sort of terms is self defined?
    1) diffuse, changing terms--------------- fixed, clearly defined
                                    terms
    2) flexible behavior--------------------- person is located in a
                                    social system

  b. Where does a person's identity seem to be?
    1) within the self (achievement)---------- outside the self in roles
                                    groups, family, clan,
                                    caste, society

  c. Nature of the individual
    1) separate aspects (intent, thought,
        act, biographical background)------- totality of person

  d. On whom should a person place reliance?
    1) self---------------------------------- status superiors, patron,
                                    others
    2) impersonal organizations--------------- persons

  e. What kind of person is valued and respected?
    What qualities?
    1) youthful (vigorous)------------------- aged (wise, experienced)

  f. What is the basis of social control?
    1) persuasion, appeal to the individual--- formal, authoritative
    2) guilt--------------------------------- shame

American	Contrast-American

Generalized Forms

a) lineal--------------------------------(time)   nonlineal

b) efficient and material cause-and-effect
   thinking-------------------------(thinking)   formal causes, correlative
       thinking

c) material, substantive------(essence and energy)   spirit, energy

d) operationalism (implied observer)-------------   direct apprehension or
       formalism (dual con-
       trast)

e) induction-------------------------------------   deduction or transduc-
       tion (dual contrast)

f) judgment by comparison------------------------   judgment against an
       absolute standard

g) world stuff expansive (unlimited good)--------   world stuff restricted
       (limited good)

Adapted from material by Edward Stewart, who wishes to acknowledge the contributions of Dr. Jasper Ingersoll, Department of Anthropology, Catholic
University,to the development of this table.

---

(17) CULTURAL VALUE SYSTEMS WITH CONFLICTING POINTS OF VIEW

OBJECTIVE

To demonstrate the contrasting and conflicting aspects of interaction
between persons who do not share the same basic assumptions.

PARTICIPANTS

Two or more persons representing different cultures. Facilitator.

MATERIALS

None.

SETTING

No special requirements.

TIME

At least one-half hour.

PROCEDURE

1) Divide into two or more individual or group units.

2) Generate alternative value systems from the members' own backgrounds (Example: a system that is property or rule oriented and one that is person oriented).

3) Assign each value system to one of the individual or group units.

4) Discuss a topic in which those value systems are likely to be contrasting or conflicting with one another.

5) Require each individual or group unit to maintain a position consistent with the assigned value system.

6) One or more observers may be assigned to take votes and referee.

7) Each group will be evaluated according to:

   a. the criteria of whether they maintained a position consistent with their assigned value system,
   b. whether they were more skillful in developing a powerful argument for their position based on these borrowed values.

Developed by Paul Pedersen, University of Minnesota.

IDENTIFICATION OF ROLES

(18) THE FISH BOWL

OBJECTIVE

To stimulate awareness of the cultural behavior of people in groups and provide feedback to group members on the roles which fellow members have perceived him/her to play.

PARTICIPANTS

Enough people representing a diversity of cultural backgrounds to form an even number of small groups of about five to six people each. Facilitator.

MATERIALS

Checklist of Observations, pencils.

SETTING

No special requirements.

TIME

At least thirty to forty-five minutes.

PROCEDURE

1) Even-numbered groups are given a problem to discuss and resolve within a limited period -- say twenty minutes. The topic selected should be one of strong current interest, controversial enough to engage all the participants.

2) Each odd-number group sits outside a group engaged in discussion and each member is confidentially assigned to watch closely the behavior of one member of the inside group, using the checklist to guide their observations.

3) After the "fish bowl" has run twenty minutes the outsiders are asked for their observations of their assigned subjects.

4) Then the subjects themselves explain why they participated in the discussion as they did, attempting to account for their behavior in cultural terms (e.g., social customs and values typifying their respective cultures).

5) Finally, the facilitator summarizes cultural differences in participant

behavior which have been demonstrated during the session.

Adapted from "The Fish Bowl" in A Manual of Teaching Techniques for Inter-cultural Education (UNESCO). October, 1971. Henry Holmes and Stephen Guild, eds.

CHECKLIST OF OBSERVATIONS

Kind of Behavior	Number of Instances Observed	Total

Task Orientation:

    Initiating

    Pushing

    Seeking Information

    Giving Information

    Seeking Opinion

    Giving Opinion

    Interrupting

    Coordinating

    Summarizing

Group Process Orientation:

    Encouraging

    Clarifying

    Expressing group feeling

Supporting

Relying on others

Deferring to others

Avoiding problems

Stressing relationships

Being aloof

---

(19) PROJECTING INTO A GROUP

OBJECTIVE

To help cross-culture workshop participants get at differences in how they see groups by providing a picture of a group whose interaction can be interpreted in a variety of ways.

PARTICIPANTS

Three or more persons. Facilitator.

MATERIALS

A copy of the group picture for each participant.

SETTING

No special requirements.

TIME

At least twenty minutes to one-half hour.

PROCEDURE

1) Copies of the picture are given to participants.

2) Each member is asked to identify the persons in the picture according to their race and give a brief description of what is happening.

3) Discuss response differences in terms of the cultural identity of the participants and the assumed roles of the picture group members.

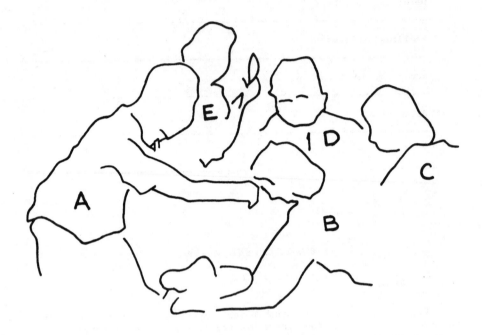

Developed by Murray Thomas, University of California, Santa Barbara.

(20) THE HIDDEN AGENDA

OBJECTIVE

To generate data early in a group meeting on the different roles cultures utilize to manage group situations and pressures.

PARTICIPANTS

Three or more persons from different cultures. Facilitator.

MATERIALS

None.

SETTING

No special requirements.

TIME

Variable. At least fifteen to twenty minutes.

PROCEDURE

1) The facilitator, knowing the members of the group, will design a list of role tasks that reflect cultural stereotypes relating to the cultural identity of persons in the group.

2) Some of these role tasks may be to always answer in the negative, or always in the positive, or to befriend one other person, or to get into an argument with one other person, or to talk a great deal of the time, or not to talk at all.

3) Each member of the group will be given a slip of paper with one role task on it which must be performed within the ten-minute group task as a committee to make a particular decision.

4) No member will be informed of what role task the other members of the group were assigned,and each member will be instructed to keep others from finding him or her out.

5) After the ten minutes are over the group members can discuss what they thought the other members' role task may have been and how performance of those role tasks affected the committee's activity.

Designed by Paul Pedersen, University of Minnesota.

(21) THE SITUATION EXERCISE

OBJECTIVE

To provide experience interacting with members of a basically unfamiliar culture.

PARTICIPANTS

Three or more persons from a culture of concern who act out a rehearsed plot while interacting with one person not from their culture who is not familiar with the plot. Facilitator.

MATERIALS

Video-tape equipment recommended. Stage-props as indicated in skit.

SETTING

Consonant with plot requirements.

TIME

At least thirty to forty-five minutes for the exercise itself.

PROCEDURE

1) A group of people from the culture being studied should be assembled. Together with the person not of their culture, the group should construct one situation which best illustrates differences between their cultures. The non-member will be expected to play himself and the situation should be one which closely approximates one he might encounter in another culture (a white youth in a black home, a Westerner in another country, etc.). The situation should pose, implicitly, some problem needing resolution.

2) Roles should be written and rehearsed with someone playing the role of the non-member, until a rough dialogue is established and coordinated with stage properties and other effects. The skit should be rehearsed a number of times, experimenting with a variety of reactions on the part of the non-member, whose behavior will be unknown and unique with each individual. The skit's length should not be longer than five to ten minutes.

3) If observers are to be permitted during the exercise, they should be positioned in such a way as to make them as inconspicuous as possible (preferably out of the line of vision of the non-member, who will perform best if not distracted).

4) The situational exercise is often conducted in the language of the culture being studied and the skit should include a high degree of non-verbal cues by the actors as well. If the non-member is unfamiliar with the language, these cues may help him in getting through the scene.

The cues are also important for the discussion which will conclude the exercise.

5) If video-tape equipment is available, the entire skit can be recorded and played back to the participants. Later, a similar skit can be staged again and by using video-tape a second time, the student can observe how his inter-cultural skills have improved.

6) Following the skit, the facilitator should allow a twenty- to thirty-minute discussion, organized around the topics given below:

  a. What was each of the people trying to accomplish?
  b. Where did the problem lie?
  c. What differences did you notice in how each one behaved in carrying out his task? What non-verbal differences did you observe?
  d. How suitable was the behavior of each person to his task?
  e. How do you think each one felt during the scene?
  f. How might you have approached the various roles?

Adapted from "The Situation Exercise" in A Manual of Teaching Techniques for Intercultural Education (UNESCO). October, 1971. Henry Holmes and Stephen Guild, eds.

---

(22) PERSONAL ROLE MODEL

OBJECTIVE

To help one assess and conceptualize his/her relationships with persons in a multi-culture group.

PARTICIPANTS

Three to ten persons. Facilitator.

MATERIALS

One copy of the Personal Role Model Scale for each participant, pencils.

SETTING

No special requirements.

TIME

Variable; at least ten minutes.

PROCEDURE

1) After a group has met several times and members have developed some
   familiarity with one another, the facilitator gives each group member
   a copy of the scale.

2) The facilitator then explains:

   a. the objective
   b. that information disclosed is considered personal which _may_ be
      shared with the group if participants choose to do so
   c. that after assessing relationships as they currently exist,partici-
      pants may wish to examine and/or disucss possible directions of
      change, development, or improvement.

    Use the following scale to assess your relationship with each person
in your Discussion Group in respect to each of the items below.

1	2	3	4	5	6	7	8
Not at all	Almost not at all	Very little	Some-what	Quite a bit	Very much	Almost com-pletely	Complete-ly

A. How free you feel to give feedback to this person.

B. How easy is it for you to accept feedback from this person.

C. How free you feel to share with this person something you feel
   you _should_ say in the group but haven't.

D. How comfortable you feel it would be to work with this person.

E. The extent to which you feel you will be able to work with this
   person to build a more effective relationship.

F. The extent to which this person has been helpful and supportive
   with you in the group.

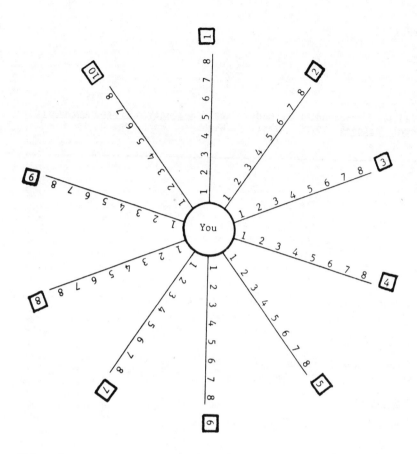

Using the scale on the preceding page and the role model above, indicate your relationship with each person on each item (A through F) by putting the appropriate number in each square below:

	1	2	3	4	5	6	7	8	9	10
A										
B										
C										
D										
E										
F										

Comments:

Adapted from "Personal Role Model" in <u>Guidelines for Peace Corps Cross-Cultural Training</u>, 1970. Albert R. Wight and Mary Anne Hammons, eds.

---

(23)   MARITAL ROLES SCALE

OBJECTIVE

Clarification of one's preferred marital roles as they pertain to his/her cultural identifications.

PARTICIPANTS

One or more persons. Facilitator if done as a group exercise. Group members should represent various cultural viewpoints.

MATERIALS

Pencils. Scales for each participant.

SETTING

No special requirements.

TIME

At least ten minutes.

PROCEDURE

1) Each participant is given a copy of the scale and a pencil.

2) Participants fill in one response before each of the following statements to indicate what they believe is right as a matter of principle. The responses are to be marked as follows:

SA -- Strongly Agree;   A -- Agree;   U -- Undecided;   D -- Disagree;

SD -- Strongly Disagree.

3) If done as a group exercise, compare and discuss responses in regard to different cultural beliefs.

_____ 1. The husband should help with the housework.

_____ 2. The wife should take a job if she wants to.

_____ 3. The husband should help wash dishes.

_____ 4. If a husband runs around, so can his wife.

_____ 5. Wives are too independent these years.

_____ 6. If the husband wants children, the wife should agree.

_____ 7. The husband should decide who is to spend the extra money.

_____ 8. Husbands should be more strict with their wives.

_____ 9. What a husband does in his spare time is his own business.

_____10. The husband should decide where to live.

_____11. The wife should fit her life to her husband's.

_____12. The husband's wishes should come first in most things.

_____13. Marriage is the best career for the woman.

_____14. The husband should wear the "pants" in the family.

_____15. If the husband is running around with another woman, his wife should put up with it until he comes to his senses.

_____16. It's okay for the wife to earn as much as her husband.

_____17. A wife should let her husband decide most things.

_____18. Almost all money matters should be decided by the husband.

(24) ORIENTATION FOR A CROSS-CULTURAL EXPERIENCE

OBJECTIVE

To help persons new to a culture define the kinds of roles they feel are important for themselves and to learn whether their suggested solutions to problems are appropriate to their new culture.

PARTICIPANTS

One or more persons. Facilitator if done as a group exercise.

MATERIALS

Pencils.

SETTING

No special requirements.

TIME

At least one hour.

PROCEDURE

1) Participants are presented with the following list of images that persons from other cultures could manifest (others may be added):

   a. Internationalist/nationalist
   b. Traditionalist/progressive
   c. Insider/visitor guest
   d. Deserving/poor
   e. Disoriented/oriented
   f. Competitor
   g. Culture sharer
   h. Elite

2) Participants select out three images which they feel are most appropriate to themselves.

3) Participants are then presented with problems and five solutions consonant with the three images they selected. They select from the five solutions the one that most appeals to them. The following are two examples of problems and solutions within the image contexts, respectively, of Insider/Visitor Guest and Disoriented/Oriented:

Example I:

A foreign student had an argument with his host family. He felt that the whole family was demanding too much of his time and attention. The family in turn felt the guest was being discourteous and demanding special treatment that they would not give to their own children. The arguments became so oppressive that they affected the student's grades.

Alternatives

1. I would make some excuse and leave the host family and find another place to live.
2. I would confront the host family and tell them they were taking too much time and tell them to give me more time to study.
3. I would rearrange my schedule and try to study more at the university and continue to let the family take up time.
4. I would do nothing and would accept it and do my best in school.
5. Or I would _____.

Example II:

A foreign person fails in his attempt to mix socially with Americans, and puts the blame on his ethnic identity. He debases the values of his own culture and rejects his countrymen, who in turn reject him. At the same time he is not more successful in communicating with Americans. He is isolated and feels lonely.

Alternatives

1. I would accept living in a foreign country and realize I will be lonely.
2. I would seek help, preferably from other countrymen and counselors.
3. I would socialize with people from my own country and try to show them the stupidity of our values.
4. I would start over and try to mix socially with another group of Americans.
5. Or I would _____.

4) Participants discuss each other's solutions in terms of whether or not they feel the solution helps or hinders the person's image and is appropriate to the situation.

5) Roles appropriate to the problems are then assigned and the problem is 'played-out.'

6) Following the role-playing, each person is allowed to defend his or her position and a vote is taken of all participants regarding the best solution.

7) Participants may then form small groups (8-10 persons) and develop their own set of problems to solve with accompanying discussion, role-playing, and voting in order to rehearse solutions to their own present and future problems.

Adapted from "Dress Rehearsal for a Cross-Cultural Experience," by R. T. Moran, Josef A. Mestenhauser and Paul B. Pedersen. International Educational and Cultural Exchange, Summer, 1974.

(25) ROLE PLAYS

OBJECTIVE

To have persons experience at first-hand many of the cultural principles which up to this moment they may have only read or discussed in fairly abstract terms.

PARTICIPANTS

No more than six observers and actors, consonant with requirements of the scenario (two or three recommended). Facilitator.

MATERIALS

Instructions for actors; Scenarios for actors and observers.

SETTING

Appropriate to scenario.

TIME

Variable. At least forty-five to sixty minutes.

PROCEDURE

1) The facilitator should review program materials and experiences and, if possible, discuss with members of the culture being studied any major cultural differences which might constitute an effective role play. He might ask for specific examples the respondents have observed in which members of another culture have come in contact with their own -- at the market, school, customs office, or social visits. Still better, identify an encounter which the training group members themselves might expect to face when they visit the unfamiliar community.

2) The trainer-leader then prepares some objectives, based partly on material previously learned and partly on goals which only the role play can offer, for example:

   a. Demonstrate an understanding of the importance of conformity and tradition
   b. Demonstrate an understanding of the value of status and respect for authority
   c. Show an awareness of different attitudes toward change and other foreign values
   d. Show skill in dealing with an official from another culture
   e. Show awareness of certain family pressures faced by the other person
   f. Demonstrate the ability to control one's own tendency to push one's own point of view; find a thoughtful compromise, and control one's frustration during the process.

3) From this information the facilitator composes a single incident on which

to build the role play. It should be a short encounter which can be "played out" in fifteen or twenty minutes.

4) The leader writes a one-paragraph general statement describing the scene (a "Scenario") for the actors and the observers.

5) He prepares short written "instructions" for the two or three partici- pants who are to join the role play. The instructions should be a paragraph or two in length and sufficiently sketchy to allow a great deal of freedom in interpretation. Each character's point of view to- ward the encounter should be described in positive terms, so that each appears to be logical in its cultural context. But the roles should be directed:

    a. toward conflicting ends or
    b. use incompatible means of achieving a common end

6) At the beginning of the session, it is especially important to try to involve all the participants, including observers, in the activity.

    a. Begin the session by saying to everyone that in a moment two of them will be chosen to play roles based on the scenario about to be handed out. "Two of you will be sitting in those two chairs."
    b. Give them a few minutes to read the scenario and discuss how they would approach each role if they were chosen to act in it.
    c. Select two members to play the roles; do not necessarily choose those who will "perform best" in the roles, but two who can benefit themselves and the observers by participating.
    d. Ask the remaining members, as they are breathing sighs of relief, to prepare to make observations on a number of points: the sources of conflict between the characters, differences in behavior (spoken and un-spoken), and feelings shown during the action.

7) After the scene has been played, allow twenty to thirty minutes for dis- cussion of it.

8) Turning finally to the actors, each one is asked to describe 1) how he felt during the session and 2) how he might have conducted himself in order to feel more comfortable and/or be more effective.

9) Be sure to tie the role play, by way of summary, to the various other activities of the inter-cultural problem. All participants are asked to take a few minutes to record what they learned from the session; optional- ly, they may volunteer to tell the group any points they have written down.

10) Variations:

    a. Use a member of the community being studied as one of the actors.
    b. Select new actors from among the observers and run through the role play again.
    c. Use video-tape equipment to record the action. Play it back to illus- trate and study particularly important gestures and issues which arose.

Adapted from "Role Plays" in A Manual of Teaching Techniques for Intercul- tural Education (UNESCO). October, 1971. Henry Holmes and Stephen Guild, eds.

(26) ROLE PLAYING A NEWSPAPER INCIDENT

OBJECTIVE

To demonstrate how persons from different backgrounds see different-ly everyday events which involve persons from more than one culture.

PARTICIPANTS

Any number of persons from a variety of cultural backgrounds who are familiar enough with one another to role play with a minimum of self-con-sciousness. Facilitator.

MATERIALS

One or more newspapers.

SETTING

No special requirements.

TIME

Variable; depending on group size and complexity of pantomine activi-ty and questioning.

PROCEDURE

1) The facilitator will bring one or more newspapers into the group and ask the members to examine the papers.

2) Group members will each select from the paper a story involving persons from several cultures with which they can identify and which could pos-sibly have happened to them personally.

3) Each member of the group will in turn project him or herself into the role of one main person in the selected story and tell the group about what happened as though it had happened to him or her personally.

4) Group members are free to ask questions of each person telling the story to explicate aspects of the story that they find difficult to understand.

Developed by Paul Pedersen, University of Minnesota.

(27) ROLE PLAYING A PROBLEM IN A GROUP

OBJECTIVE

To allow a group an opportunity to project themselves into a cross-cultural problem, rather than discussion of a problem, by assuming roles of persons involved in that problem, not necessarily their own culture roles.

PARTICIPANTS

Any number of persons to assume "problem" and "observer" roles. Facilitator.

MATERIALS

None.

SETTING

Enough open space to allow for whatever role playing activities may emerge.

TIME

Variable; depending on the length and complexity of the role playing session and processing phase.

PROCEDURE

A problem-solving format would be helpful to get at an ambiguous problem or crisis area in the group's discussion, especially when the group is divided on an issue and unable to come to a resolution.

1) A group member or the facilitator can ask that the group divide up into roles to "do" a cross-cultural problem, which may be from his own background or in some other way related to the group. A problem may have already emerged in the group discussion.

2) The members of the group divide up available roles in working with the problem.

3) Members of the group select roles in which they will participate in a group role play situation, which may be from their own culture or a contrasting culture.

4) One or more members will remain in the role of an observer or referee to facilitate debriefing.

5) The members will then act out in their assumed roles the conflict situation of the selected problem.

6) After role playing members will be asked to tell the group what they

learned about the problem.

Developed by Paul Pedersen, University of Minnesota.

GROUP PROCESS

(28) GROUP FUNCTION REVIEW

OBJECTIVE

To determine how persons in the role of cross-culture group leader perceive matters of importance on four different levels.

PARTICIPANTS

One or more persons who function as group leaders.

MATERIALS

Pencils.

SETTING

No special requirements.

TIME

Variable; at least five to ten minutes.

PROCEDURE

1) List under the following headings the most valuable one thing, in your judgment, that happened during the group meeting.

A. to the group

B. to you as a leader

C. to a particular member

D. to illustrate cultural differences or similarities

2) List under the following headings the least valuable one thing, in your judgment, that happened during the group meeting.

A. to the group

B. to you as a leader

C. to a particular member

D. to illustrate cultural differences or similarities

(29) INTERIM OBJECTIVES ASSESSMENT SCALE

OBJECTIVE

To assess the extent to which interim objectives - upon which the attainment of final objectives hinges - have been achieved in a group of mixed-culture membership.

PARTICIPANTS

Three to ten persons. Facilitator.

MATERIALS

One copy of the Interim Objective Assessment Scale for each participant. Pencils.

SETTING

No special requirements.

TIME

Variable. At least ten minutes.

PROCEDURE

1) The facilitator gives a copy of the scale and a pencil to each group member.

2) The facilitator then explains:

a. the objective of the rating
b. that members' responses will be considered by the entire group for the purpose of enhancing progress toward final group goals.

Suggested interim objectives for a group are that each participant:

A. Become actively involved in the experiential learning process.

B. Demonstrate a willingness to risk, to be open, and to expose himself, rather than to maintain a protective wall around himself.

C. Demonstrate the willingness and ability to own up to his own behavior, accepting and acting upon feedback from others nondefensively.

D. Take responsibility for the group and its members by openly sharing information with one another and giving useful feedback.

Using the following scale, indicate the extent to which you feel you and the other members of your group have been able to achieve these interim learning objectives.

not at all

completely

| 1 | 2 | 3 | 4 | 5 | 6 | 7 | 8 | 9 |

Participants*

ITEMS										
A										
B										
C										
D										

Why do you think the group has developed in this manner?

*Write in each participant's D-Group number in the box at the top of each column.

Adapted from "Interim Objectives Assessment Scale" in Guidelines for Peace Corps Cross-Cultural Training, 1970. Albert R. Wight and Mary Anne Hammons, eds.

(30)   THE MOON SURVIVAL PROBLEM

OBJECTIVE

To demonstrate the advantage in most instances of group task decisions over individual task decisions if participants overcome differences such as those which may result from cultural dissimilarity.

PARTICIPANTS

Three or more persons representing varied cultural backgrounds. Facilitator.

MATERIALS

Rank order sheets and pencils for each participant.

SETTING

No special requirements.

TIME

Five to ten minutes to read instructions and perform individual rankings. At least ten to twenty minutes for team phase and discussion of results.

PROCEDURE

The situation described in this problem is imaginary. Your "life" or "death" will depend upon how well your group can share its present knowledge of a relatively unfamiliar problem so that the team can make decisions that will lead to your survival.

1) You are a member of a space crew drawn from several earth countries participating in a United Nations inner-galactic science project. Originally, your vessel was scheduled to rendezvous with a mother ship on the lighted surface of the moon. Due to mechanical difficulties, however, your ship was forced to land at a spot some 300 kilometers from the meeting point. You were unable to notify anyone of your position before the forced landing. None of you are injured and your space suits are intact.

However, during landing, much of the equipment aboard was damaged, but your group was able to salvage the fifteen items listed on the next page. Since survival depends on reaching the mother ship, the most critical items available must be chosen for the 300-kilometer trip.

You may assume:

A. the number of your crew is the same as the number on your team
B. you are the actual people in the situation
C. the team has agreed to stick together
D. all items are in good condition

E. you are on the lighted side of the moon.

2) Each member of the team is to individually rank the fifteen salvaged items according to their importance to the team's survival. Do not discuss the situation or problem until each member has finished the individual ranking.

3) After everyone has finished the individual ranking, rank order the fifteen items as a team. Once discussion begins do not change your individual ranking.

    Your team will have until _____ o'clock to complete this step.

4) Discuss the data in regard to the objective.

Adapted from "NASA Exercise" in The Dynamics of Human Communication (A Laboratory Approach). Gail E. Myers and Michele Tolela Myers.

	STEP 1 Your Individual Ranking	STEP 2 The Team's Ranking	STEP 3 Survival Expert's Ranking	STEP 4 Difference Between Steps 1 & 3	STEP 5 Difference Between Steps 2 & 3
box of matches			15		
food concentrate			4		
50 ft. nylon rope			6		
parachute silk			8		
portable heating unit			13		
two .45 caliber pistols			11		
one case dehydrated milk			12		
two 100 lbs. tank of oxygen			1		
stellar map (of moon's constellation)			3		
life raft			9		
magnetic compass			14		
5 gallons of water			2		
signal flares			10		
first aid kit with injection needles			7		
solar-powered FM receiver-transmitter			5		
			TOTALS (the lower the score the better)	Your Score Step 4	Your Score Step 5

Step 6   AVERAGE INDIVIDUAL SCORE
add up all the individual scores (Step 4) on the team and divide by the number on the team.

Step 8   LOWEST INDIVIDUAL SCORE on the team

Step 7   GAIN SCORE
Difference between Step 5 and Step 6. If Step 5 is lower than Step 6, gain is "+"; otherwise, gain is "-".

Step 9   NUMBER OF INDIVIDUAL scores LOWER than the team score

(31) RESPONSIBLE FEEDBACK

OBJECTIVE

To increase cross-cultural workshop participants' understanding of the nature and importance of feedback, and how to give, receive, and use responsible feedback.

PARTICIPANTS

At least two groups of ten persons of different cultural backgrounds. One facilitator for each group.

MATERIALS

A copy of Characteristics of Effective Feedback for each participant. One or more group process questionnaires for each group.

SETTING

Several adjoining rooms that participants may use for group experiences, filling out questionnaires, and for skit preparation. One large room with open floor space for skit presentation and follow-up discussion and assessment. Writing surfaces and movable chairs for each participant are desirable.

TIME

Two full consecutive days are recommended.

PROCEDURE

1) Participants should engage in several group experiences and fill out two or more group process questionnaires. Feedback issues are then discussed.

2) Participants are given copies of Characteristics of Effective Feedback and told that their group is to prepare brief role playing skits to demonstrate the right way and wrong way to give feedback, based on the examples given in the handout.

3) The next day some time is allowed for skit preparation. Then, each group should present its skits to the total community, or, if the community is too large, to two or three other groups.

4) Following skit presentation, facilitators should conduct a discussion relating the skits to the handout and to other session discussions, exercises, evaluations, and assessments.

5) Facilitators should reinforce positive attitudes toward feedback and work with those participants who are having difficulty accepting and understanding the concept. Facilitators should work together to provide timely, meaningful, and honest feedback to the participants.

6) An alternative to this way of conducting the exercise is to have the group role play effective and ineffective ways of providing feedback for each of the ten suggestions without preparing skits. Facilitators might rotate through the groups to see how they are doing, to provide encouragement and support, and to answer questions about the exercise.

Characteristics of effective feedback:*

1. It is <u>specific</u> rather than general. To be told that one is "dominating" will probably not be as useful as to be told that "Just now you were not listening to what the others said, but I felt I had to agree with your arguments or face attack from you."

2. It is <u>focused</u> <u>on</u> <u>behavior</u> rather than on the person. It is important that we relate to <u>what</u> <u>a</u> <u>person</u> <u>does</u> rather than to what we think or imagine he is. Thus we might say that a person "talked more than anyone else in this meeting" rather than that he is "a loudmouth." The former allows for the possibility of change; the latter implies a fixed personality trait.

3. It takes into account the <u>needs</u> <u>of</u> <u>the</u> <u>receiver</u> of the feedback. Feedback can be destructive when it serves only our own needs and fails to consider the needs of the person on the receiving end. It should be given to help, not to hurt. We too often give feedback because it makes us feel better or gives us a psychological advantage.

4. It is directed toward <u>behavior</u> <u>which</u> <u>the</u> <u>receiver</u> <u>can</u> <u>do</u> <u>something</u> <u>about</u>. Frustration is only increased when a person is reminded of some short-comings over which he has no control or a physical characteristic which he can do nothing about.

5. It is <u>solicited</u>, rather than imposed. Feedback is most useful when the receiver himself has formulated the kind of question which those observing him can answer or when he actively seeks feedback.

6. It involves <u>sharing</u> <u>of</u> <u>information</u> rather than giving advice. By sharing information, we leave a person free to decide for himself, in accordance with his own goals, needs, etc. When we give advice we tell him what to do, and to some degree take away his freedom to decide for himself.

7. It is well-timed. In general, immediate feedback is most useful (depending, of course, on the person's readiness to hear it, support available from others, etc.). The recognition and use of feedback involves many possible emotional reactions. Excellent feedback presented at an inappropriate time may do more harm than good.

8. It involves <u>the</u> <u>amount</u> <u>of</u> <u>information</u> <u>the</u> <u>receiver</u> <u>can</u> <u>use</u> rather than the amount we would like to give. To overload a person with feedback is to reduce the possibility that he may be able to use what he received effectively. When we give more than can be used, we are more often than not satisfying some need of our own rather than helping the other person.

9. It concerns <u>what</u> <u>is</u> <u>said</u> <u>or</u> <u>done</u>, <u>or</u> <u>how</u>, <u>not</u> <u>why</u>. The "why"

takes us from the observable to the inferred and involves assumptions regarding motive or intent. Telling a person what his motivations or inten-
tions are more often than not tends to alienate the person, and contributes
to a climate of resentment, suspicion, and distrust; it does not contribute
to learning or development. It is dangerous to assume that we know why a
person says or does something, or what he "really" means, or what he is
"really" trying to accomplish. If we are uncertain of his motives or intent, this uncertainty itself is feedback, however, and should be revealed.

10. It is checked to insure clear communication. One way of doing
this is to have the receiver try to rephrase the feedback he has received
to see if it corresponds to what the sender had in mind. No matter what
the intent, feedback is often threatening and thus subject to considerable
distortion or misinterpretation.

*Original list brainstormed by George Lehner and Al Wight in 1963.

Adapted from "Responsible Feedback" in Guidelines for Peace Corps Cross-
Cultural Training, 1970. Albert R. Wight and Mary Anne Hammons, eds.

---

(32) ANONYMOUS FEEDBACK FROM THE GROUP

OBJECTIVE

To provide anonymous feedback to all the members of one culture in a
group through group discussion about that individual or group without that
individual or group being present.

PARTICIPANTS

Any number of persons representing a variety of cultures. Facilitator.

MATERIALS

None.

SETTING

No special requirements.

TIME

Variable, depending on group size and time allotted for discussion
of members.

PROCEDURE

This exercise violates many entrenched taboos in our society about gossip. If it is used it would have to have the full agreement of all members and assume complete confidentiality. The facilitator would have to be very careful that individual members were not placed under more stress than they could tolerate.

1) Ask each individual or sub-group from each culture area to leave the room for a given period of time. Dyads are safer than individuals, giving the exercise less of a threatening or rejecting appearance.

2) While the individual or sub-group is out of the room the group discusses that individual or group providing both positive and negative feedback and coming to some balanced consensus or range of opinions about the missing member.

3) The member or members are asked to come back into the room and someone such as the facilitator tells them what the group said about them while they were gone.

4) The identity of persons making individual comments should be kept confidential unless that person chooses to reveal himself.

Developed by Paul Pedersen, University of Minnesota.

---

(33) HOW AM I DOING?

OBJECTIVE

To help assess the performance of the cross-culture group one leads and evaluate oneself in the group.

PARTICIPANTS

One or more persons.

MATERIALS

Pencils.

SETTING

No special requirements.

<u>TIME</u>

At least five minutes.

<u>PROCEDURE</u>

1) Check off those items relevant to your group's performance and to your own performance in the group.

2) Discuss your ratings with another participant for the purpose of improving group functioning.

HOW AM I DOING?

Checklist of Favorable Symptoms

Members address me no more formally than others in group.

Members frequently express real feelings.

Group starts itself at beginning of each meeting.

Sometimes members openly disagree with me.

Members address their remarks to each other rather than to me.

Group has a tendency to want to remain after the time limit has been passed.

Group makes decisions without depending on me as the final judge.

Members seem to know what goals they seek.

Members speak up without asking for my permission.

Members do not count on me alone to handle "problem members."

"Bright ideas" originate with many members of the group.

Different individuals frequently lead the group's thinking, discussion and procedure.

Members seem to listen to each other without interrupting.

Conflicts and disagreements frequently arise, but people try to understand the nature of these and deal with them.

Members often accept insights and information from other members.

There is an absence of hostility toward me.

Members draw out and question each other to better understand their contributions.

(34) GROUP EXPERIENCE SELF-DISCOVERY TEST

OBJECTIVE

To specify how members of a cross-culture group perceive themselves functioning in the group.

PARTICIPANTS

One or more persons.

MATERIALS

Pencils.

SETTING

No special requirements.

TIME

At least three to five minutes.

PROCEDURE

1) On each of the following five items participants check (✓) the point on each line where their feelings are most nearly described.

2) If done as a group exercise, responses may be made public and discussed for thé purpose of clarifying to the group how members view themselves and to clarify to the members how the group views them in relation to their self-views.

GROUP EXPERIENCE
Self-Discovery List

1. ACCEPTING AND UNDERSTANDING OTHERS IN GROUPS:

1	2	3	4	5
I am critical and caustic, disregarding feelings of others.	I am frequently indifferent to what others are saying.	I listen to what others say but am not aware of their real feelings.	I try to listen with openness and expectancy to others' feelings as well as to their ideas.	I am able to accept and understand some of the reasons for others feeling as they do.

2. BEING ACCEPTED AND UNDERSTOOD:

1	2	3	4	5
In groups, I am afraid if I speak up my ideas would appear feeble or irrelevant.	At times, in groups, I feel ignored or judged and am defensive.	I usually feel a part of a group but not free to say what I really think.	I feel free to express myself in a group. Some members try to listen with openness and expectancy.	I feel free to express my real self when in a group and feel considerable group understanding and acceptance.

3. VERBAL COMMUNICATING:

1	2	3	4	5
In groups I often interrupt others, interjecting irrelevant ideas.	I feel I usually talk too much in groups.	In groups, I make an effort to curb my talking.	In groups, I hold back my ideas until the appropriate time.	I feel a responsibility to allow others to express their ideas in groups.

4. PARTICIPATING IN GROUPS:

1	2	3	4	5
In groups, I usually feel like an observer.	I become slightly involved in groups.	I enter into group discussions primarily to convince others of my position.	I enter group discussions primarily to "work through" the concern with others.	I feel involved in groups trying to help others clarify their feelings just the same as I try to make clear my own convictions.

5. SELF-DISCOVERY AND CHANGE:

1	2	3	4	5
I feel no encounter or challenge in groups. Ideas seem on the sur-face.	I feel a little personal encounter or communion in groups but feel pressured to change against my will.	In most groups I feel intellectual and spiritual en-counter but not enough to spark me to new self-discovery.	In many groups I feel some encounter and/or communion and am free to look at myself and to think through a change.	New insights for personal growth, understanding and change come to me in groups.

(35) RECOGNITION OF FEELINGS AND ATTITUDES

IMMEDIATE FEELINGS

OBJECTIVE

To demonstrate to a cross-culture group each individual's immediate feelings about what is happening in the group through some non-verbal pantomime of activity.

PARTICIPANTS

Three or more persons from different cultures. Facilitator.

MATERIALS

None.

SETTING

No special requirements.

TIME

Variable.

PROCEDURE

1) Particularly when a group is just starting out or when the group has been engaged in intense and difficult discussion about an issue of conflict and where the persons involved are less able to express their true feelings in English than in their native language:

   A. The facilitator will stop discussion when the group has hit a deadlock over an issue it is unable to resolve.

   B. He will then instruct one or two key individuals to pantomime their feelings to the group in some non-verbal way that will communicate to the group how they feel.

   C. Others in the group will be encouraged to pick up the action and provide their own pantomime.

Designed by Robert Moran, University of Minnesota.

(36)   SPEAKING WITHOUT SPEAKING

OBJECTIVE

To demonstrate some non-verbal behaviors which are common between cultures, some which differ across cultures, and the meanings and feelings they usually communicate.

PARTICIPANTS

Two equal size groups of three or more persons each. Facilitator.

MATERIALS

None required.

SETTING

A room large enough to allow for some separation between the two groups.

TIME

Approximately one hour.

PROCEDURE

1) The facilitator may announce to participants that this session will deal with culture or even with communication; but he does not mention its focus on non-verbal behavior, lest the impact of the exercise be reduced. He then asks the participants to split into two groups of equal size, A's and B's, who then assemble at opposite ends of the room.

2) The facilitator first goes over to the A group. He tells them in a confidential voice that they are to choose a partner from the B group and engage in conversation. The subject of the conversation is not too important; it may be differences the partners may have noticed in the treatment of women in different cultures, different attitudes toward work and professional life, or some of the problems that interfere with good communication. It is essential however that during the conversation, each "A" will sit or stand about 4 inches closer to B than he normally would. All other behavior should be normal -- even the voice should be at the normal pitch.

3) The facilitator now joins the B group, telling them in a confidential voice that they are to discuss the chosen subject with one of the A group, that the A's will come over to select them shortly.

4) Next the partners are asked to meet and go to separate parts of the room, relax, and exchange views on the chosen subject. They should not go out of sight of the facilitator.

5) After about five to ten minutes the facilitator apologizes for breaking

into the conversation and asks the A's and B's to return to their respective groups. He joins the B group this time and asks in a low voice, "Without looking back at your partner, each of you tell the others in this group, as best you can, what your partner "A" looked like. For example, did he wear glasses or not? Moustache? Complexion? What kind of clothes? Neat or sloppy? Long or short hair?" Each is asked to share with his group whatever details he can recall.

6) Meanwhile the facilitator returns to the "A" group. He asks them the same question about what they can recall about their partners' appearance. He gives a few minutes for them to begin to share recollections but then apologizes and breaks in.

7) He tells the "A" group that he next wants them to engage in a second conversation with their partners. Another subject is assigned to them to discuss. This time the "A's" are told to avoid looking directly into their partners' faces; look any where that seems natural except their faces. All other behaviors should be normal.

8) The facilitator now asks the participants to rejoin their partners and he reiterates the subject they are to discuss. After five to ten minutes he again interrupts and asks them to gather, this time as a single group. He then asks for volunteers to describe how they felt during your exchange, "Did you somehow feel strange?" A brief discussion, about ten minutes, should be encouraged. Finally, the facilitator admits to everyone the instructions that he had been giving the "A" group and offers a short lecture concerning the significance of non-verbal communication.

9) Lastly, participants are asked to demonstrate examples for a discussion of specific differences in non-verbal behavior which they have noticed among themselves and other cultural groups.

Suggested by Melvin L. Schnapper to Henry Holmes and Stephen Guild, eds., A Manual of Teaching Techniques for Intercultural Education (UNESCO), October, 1971.

(37) CROSS-CULTURE ENCOUNTER REVIEW

OBJECTIVE

To clarify one's feelings in regard to a prior cross-cultural encounter.

PARTICIPANTS

One or more persons. Facilitator if done as a group exercise.

MATERIALS

Pencils.

SETTING

No special requirements.

TIME

At least three to five minutes.

PROCEDURE

1) Examine the following pairs of adjectives. If the adjective at the extreme left describes your feelings circle the number '1'. If the adjective at the extreme right describes your feelings, encircle the number '7'. If neither extreme describes your feeling, encircle the appropriate number in between.

2) If more than one participant, discuss your responses.

Pleasant	1	2	3	4	5	6	7	Unpleasant
Friendly	1	2	3	4	5	6	7	Unfriendly
Accepting	1	2	3	4	5	6	7	Rejecting
Enthusiastic	1	2	3	4	5	6	7	Unenthusiastic
Lots of fun	1	2	3	4	5	6	7	Serious
Relaxed	1	2	3	4	5	6	7	Tense
Cooperative	1	2	3	4	5	6	7	Uncooperative
Supporting	1	2	3	4	5	6	7	Hostile
Interesting	1	2	3	4	5	6	7	Boring
Harmonious	1	2	3	4	5	6	7	Quarrelsome

Self-assured	1	2	3	4	5	6	7		Hesitant
Efficient	1	2	3	4	5	6	7		Inefficient
Open	1	2	3	4	5	6	7		Guarded

Developed by Paul Torrance, University of Georgia.

---

(38) DIALOGUE WITHIN OURSELVES

OBJECTIVE

To gain practice in listening to and making cultural interpretations of 'internal dialogue' on a given cross-culture issue that generates ambivalent thoughts and feelings.

PARTICIPANTS

One person.

MATERIALS

Pencil and paper.

SETTING

A private, quiet place with a writing surface.

TIME

No limit.

PROCEDURE

1) Select a cross-culture subject which produces ambivalent thoughts and feelings within you (e.g. United States' dependence on Middle Eastern oil).

2) Tune in on your ambivalent thoughts and listen to the two sides of your internal dialogue.

3) Write down as a script of a play or conversation the dialogue between your internal voices, attempting to identify the emergence of cultural bias.

(39) WE AND YOU

OBJECTIVE

To identify inter-group culture-based perceptions and stereotypes.

PARTICIPANTS

A group of eight to fifteen persons over twelve years of age and of mixed cultural backgrounds is recommended. Facilitator.

MATERIALS

Questionnaire (prepared by facilitator along suggested lines), pencils.

SETTING

No special requirements.

TIME

At least sixty minutes.

PROCEDURE

1) The facilitator prepares a questionnaire to focus on issues which contrast the cultures being examined. The group may participate in selection of issues. The following are examples:

Attitudes toward - man's basic nature; control on one's environment; women; work; change life; authority; material objects; science; technology; time; death; achievement; value of experience; old people; strangers; status; relationships between sexes; dating; under-dogs; homosexuals; meeting commitments; government bureaucracy; classroom discipline; children being brought up to be independent.

Three questions are asked relating to each issue: How each participant

a) Thinks most people from the "other" culture feel about the issue in question.
b) Thinks most people from his own culture feel.
c) How he himself feels about it.

Each question is answered on a scale from 1 - 9 representing opposite extremes, and the individual must identify his (pre) conceptions of both cultures and his own feelings by one number on the scale. A typical attitude statement might be:

Most Mexican Americans	Most White Americans	Myself	
			1. Believe that man's basic nature is
			Basically Good/Basically Evil
_____	_____	_____	1 2 3 4 5 6 7 8 9

2) Each participant is given a copy of the finished questionnaire. Working alone for fifteen to twenty minutes participants answer all questions.

3) Participants form into small groups and try to reach a consensus (one number) upon their conceptions of each culture. This focuses the group's attention on real differences. The exercise ends when each group has reached consensus on all items, or when an arbitrary time limit is reached. (Individuals are not asked to reach consensus on their own perceptions.)

4) Historical or social analysis of attitudes expressed during the exercise may be made in conclusion.

Adapted from "We and You" in A Manual of Teaching Techniques for Intercultural Education (UNESCO), October, 1971. Henry Holmes and Stephen Guild, eds.

---

(40) PERCEPTUAL SET EXERCISE

OBJECTIVE

To demonstrate to people how easily their perceptions of another person can be influenced; that their perceptions are probably never completely free from culture bias; and the importance of being open to experience.

PARTICIPANTS

At least 15 persons divided into three equal groups. Facilitator. Guest speaker.

MATERIALS

Questionnaires, pencils.

SETTING

A separate room for each group and a general meeting room.

TIME

Variable. At least one to two hours.

PROCEDURE

1) A guest speaker, someone the participants have not met, is asked to address the participants. He should be told beforehand the nature and purpose of the exercise and to hold his talk to not more than fifteen or twenty minutes. He should also be told that he will be given additional time with the participants after the exercise.

2) Before the speaker arrives, the participants should be divided into three equal groups for some planned activity. At the end of this group activity, the groups are instructed to go directly to the general meeting room for a presentation by a guest speaker. The groups, however, are given three different "sets:" One group will receive a positive set, one a negative set, and one a neutral set.

A. The sets should be written out beforehand, gone over, and rehearsed by those staff members who will be giving the sets, so that strong and credible positive and negative sets are given.

B. The negative set should present a very negative picture of the individual - that he is a phony, a politician, two-faced, pompous, self-centered, defensive, a manipulator, anything that is plausible but negative. Ideally, it should cover many of the same characteristics in the questionnaire but in different words.

C. The positive set should be the opposite of the negative set. He is warm, sincere, honest, generous, understanding, etc. Again, it should not be so strong that it becomes suspect, but strong enough to give the picture of a really great guy.

D. The neutral set is in a sense no set at all. The group is simply instructed to report to the general assembly for a presentation. The topic can be given, but nothing should be said about the speaker.

E. Timing should be such that the participants proceed directly to the general assembly, so that members of different groups will not have an opportunity to discuss their different sets.

3) Immediately following the presentation, the participants are asked to complete a questionnaire reporting their impressions of the speaker. They should be asked to complete the questionnaire as quickly as possible and to be as honest as possible in checking the alternative that most closely matches their impressions, granting that these are only initial impressions. They should be told that the purpose of the questionnaire will be explained when the data are fed back.

4) For feedback when the entire group is assembled, the data should either be run off on ditto or recorded on a blackboard or large newsprint sheets. The data should speak for itself.

5) In relation to the exercise objective, implications of the exercise are discussed.

Name_____

Group #_____

DIRECTIONS

On the basis of your impressions of this person, check one alternative in each set which you feel would most accurately describe him. Work quickly, and check the alternative that most closely matches your impression.

1. In general, how does he get along with other people?
_____a. very well, with close friends, but only if he knows them well
_____b. people are impressed until they really get to know him
_____c. is well liked, meets people easily
_____d. is respected rather than liked

2. What does his attitude toward others seem to be?
_____a. is cold and distant
_____b. is somewhat indifferent to others
_____c. really likes others, enjoys meeting them
_____d. tends to take advantage of people, uses people

3. How responsive to people is he?
_____a. often is reserved and aloof, somewhat distant
_____b. very warm and open with almost everyone
_____c. a little distrustful of people, always on guard
_____d. attempts to be "warm," but really isn't

4. How would his temperament best be described?
_____a. somewhat excitable and emotional
_____b. serious, cautious
_____c. cool, calculating
_____d. tends to be a stable person, calm, easy-going

5. How might he behave in an argument?
_____a. remains calm, reasonable, and controlled
_____b. agrees on the surface, but is quite rigid
_____c. may side with other's point of view to avoid a scene
_____d. becomes angry, belligerent

6. How would he react to criticism?
_____a. shows resentment
_____b. ignores it
_____c. outwardly accepts it, but inwardly seeks revenge
_____d. is hurt, very sensitive, but keeps it to himself

7. What is his greatest strength?
_____a. loyalty, trustworthiness
_____b. sense of humor, keen wit
_____c. intelligence
_____d. shrewdness

8. What is his primary life goal?
____a. to have enough security and be comfortable
____b. to help others (e.g., the poor, the ill), to be a "good samaritan"
____c. success and recognition
____d. to receive high esteem from others

9. What about himself is he most proud of?
____a. intelligence
____b. ability to understand people
____c. sincerity, honesty
____d. ability to manipulate people

DIRECTIONS

Check one adjective or phrase in each pair which best describes the person you have just heard.

1. ____a. concerned with self
   ____b. concerned with others

11. ____a. tolerant
    ____b. prejudiced

2. ____a. sense of humor
   ____b. stern, business-like

12. ____a. conscientious
    ____b. self-centered

3. ____a. sincere
   ____b. phony

13. ____a. intelligent
    ____b. shrewd

4. ____a. suspicious
   ____b. trusting

14. ____a. optimistic
    ____b. realistic

5. ____a. vindictive
   ____b. forgiving

15. ____a. honest
    ____b. untrustworthy

6. ____a. dependable
   ____b. undependable

16. ____a. kind
    ____b. inconsiderate

7. ____a. progressive
   ____b. conservative

17. ____a. opinionated, dogmatic
    ____b. flexible, open

8. ____a. scheming
   ____b. humble

18. ____a. warm, friendly
    ____b. cold, indifferent

9. ____a. congruent
   ____b. two-faced

19. ____a. selfish
    ____b. generous

10. ____a. condescending
    ____b. considerate

20. Would you like to get to know him better?
    ____a. Yes
    ____b. No

Adapted from "Perceptual Set Exercise" in Guidelines for Peace Corps Cross-Cultural Training, 1970. Albert R. Wight and Mary Anne Hammons, eds.

(41) STEREOTYPES

OBJECTIVE

To demonstrate stereotypic attitudes held toward different groups of people.

PARTICIPANTS

One or more persons. Facilitator if done as a group exercise.

MATERIALS

Pencils.

SETTING

No special requirements.

TIME

At least ten to fifteen minutes.

PROCEDURE

1) List five different cultures within your discussion group and rank order them in conjunction with the statements below. Add up the total score for each statement on each ethnic group.

2) Address your rankings with at least the following questions:

   A. Why does stereotyping persist? Is it useful? Harmful? What kind of situations tend to stereotype people?

   B. If several persons undertook this exercise, what similarities in ratings exist? Were there few or different answers to each item? Are there any sex and age differences noted in the ratings?

Groups					
A	B	C	D	E	statements
					not at all aggressive
					conceited about appearance
					very ambitious
					almost always acts as a leader
					very independent
					does not hide emotions at all
					sneaky
					cried easily
					very active
					very logical
					not at all competitive
					feelings easily hurt
					not at all emotional
					very strong need for security
					easily influenced
					very objective
					very self-confident
					easy going
					has difficulty making decisions
					dependent
					likes math and science very much
					very passive
					very direct
					knows the way of the world
					excitable in a minor crisis

A	B	C	D	E	statements
					very adventurous
					very submissive
					hard working, industrious
					not comfortable about being aggressive

---

(42) A STUDY OF PHYSICAL COMMUNICATION: THE HAND

OBJECTIVE

To specify the affective correlates of certain physical gestures and the differences of interpretation which exist across cultures.

PARTICIPANTS

One or more persons. If done as a group exercise, a facilitator should be present and group members should represent different cultures.

MATERIALS

Pencils. Copies of The Hand grid for each participant.

SETTING

No special requirements.

TIME

Variable. At least five to ten minutes.

PROCEDURE

1) Participants should receive a pencil and one copy of The Hand grid.

2) In terms of each participant's observation of his own behavior they are to indicate what they feel is appropriate and typical physical use of the hand, according to the affective category headings, by placing a + in the box when they feel the behavior is typical and a - in the box when they feel the behavior is not typical.

	Sympathy	Affection	Excitement	Hostility	Attention	Ritual
Hand to Hand						
Hand to Shoulder						
Hand to Arm						
Hand to Hip						
Hand to Face						
Hand to Head						
Hand to Knee						

Developed by Sheri Wilson and Kent Warren, University of Minnesota.

(43) LUMP SUM

OBJECTIVE

To demonstrate feelings, roles and attitudes in a simulated situation of conflict among competing national interest groups.

PARTICIPANTS

Size of groups may range from four to twelve individuals and the number of groups from four to six, each group representing a different culture. Facilitator.

MATERIALS

The simulated lump-sum of money should be adequate to stimulate planning within groups and competition between groups. Recommended is 100,000,000 units in either U.S. $ or mixed currency representing the groups' national compositions.

SETTING

Simulated international convocation. Participant countries vie for aid from the United Nations' Special Fund, the International Monetary Fund, or some other reasonably authentic donor.
Refer to appendix #1 for recommended seating arrangements.

TIME

1½ hours plus debriefing and preparation.

PROCEDURE

1) The facilitator will decide on the situation to be simulated, consulting participants if and whenever possible.

2) Participants are introduced to the interaction by the facilitator and are given a copy of the scenario to study. (See model; appendix #2.)

3) "Interest groups" are formed either through assignment of roles by the instructor or by allowing participants to volunteer for membership in designated special interest groups, keeping all groups approximately equal in size.

4) Special interest groups meet separately to:

A. Elect a special interest group negotiator,
B. Decide on the <u>overall</u> division of funds with special attention to the sum their interest group plans to request for itself and to prepare an argument defending their allocation both for all groups in general, and for their own group in particular,
C. Decide on a strategy for securing their portion, i.e., the maximum they hope to obtain and the minimum for which they will settle in

later negotiations,

D. Decide on bargaining strategies and possible coalitions of interest between groups to their mutual benefit,

E. Groups may be allowed a minimum of twenty minutes and a maximum of an hour in which to develop their initial program strategy. The longer a group meets in its initial session the stronger group identity tends to become and the less likely the group is to compromise. Since more learning seems to occur among groups which do not compromise, and thus lose the money, the more time individual groups can have in the initial session the better.

5) The first negotiation session will take place with each group's elected negotiator being placed at a bargaining table in such a way that he faces his constituency as indicated in two model seating arrangements enclosed. Each negotiator will be given only three minutes to report on his delegation's specific proposal for allocation of the money. There must be no discussion among the representatives or debate from the floor while each negotiator defends his allocation within the three minutes.

6) The first consultation session will allow negotiators to return to their group and consult with the special interest group (his own and others if desired) on strategy, presentation, and changes in the group proposal. The consultation will continue for ten minutes. Private consultation and negotiations with other special interest groups will be permitted at this time.

7) The second negotiation will bring negotiators back to the bargaining table for at least ten minutes but no more than fifteen minutes. This will be the first public bargaining session where negotiators will be allowed to speak and debate without restriction.

8) The second and last consultation session allows negotiators to return to their groups for ten minutes. In the second consultation further modifications in each group's proposals can be made. Again, each group may wish to engage in private negotiations with other groups to secure their cooperation toward a solution.

9) The third negotiation session will bring negotiators back to the bargaining table for the last time in a twenty-minute period, unless the negotiators come to a unanimous agreement before that time. Negotiators must reach unanimous agreement in this session or lose the money.

10) Following the simulation, a minimum of twenty minutes must be allowed for debriefing on the learning which has taken place through the simulation. Discussion should be oriented to the content level (articulation of information and the position of each simulated interest group by participants) and the process level (the interaction of individuals in this simulation as they approach bargaining negotiations and exercise power).

APPENDIX 1

TWO ALTERNATIVE SEATING ARRANGEMENTS FOR "LUMP-SUM"

First alternative seating arrangement:

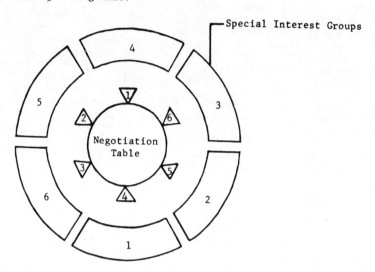

Second alternative seating arrangement:

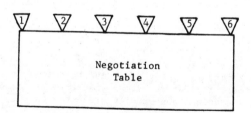

APPENDIX 2

"LUMP-SUM" SAMPLE SCENARIO

Instructions for Instructors: The following scenario is one which was used for a simulation done with students of education at the University of Malaya late in 1969. Six groups, representing the states of Malaysia, were used in that game. It is suggested that this scenario be adapted to the specifics of the simulation you will run and that you distribute copies of your adaption to each of the participants. If duplication facilities are not available, you can read your adaptation to the entire group. The words in brackets should be changed by you to suit the circumstances of the simula-tion, as you are playing it. That is, if the setting of the simulation, as you will play it, is special interest groups in New York instead of the title being "Emergency Meeting of Representatives from State Assemblies in Educa-tion Planning for Malaysia" (as it reads on the scenario presented below) you might entitle your scenario "Emergency Meeting of Representatives of Special Interest Groups in New York," etc.

In the scenario below, participants were divided into six groups, and were then presented with the scenario. That entire simulation was conducted in one day. If you should decide to play the game over two days you may do so. You should also adjust the timetable to suit the time constraints under which you may have to operate, with one session devoted to preparation and a later session devoted to negotiations.

If the simulation is being conducted in a language other than English, you should, of course, translate the scenario into the language in which the game will be conducted.

Sample Scenario

Special   STRICTLY CONFIDENTIAL

EMERGENCY MEETING OF REPRESENTATIVES FROM (STATE ASSEMBLIES ON EDUCATIONAL PLANNING FOR MALAYSIA)

You have been called together in this special emergency meeting to represent the unique interests of your (constituencies) in making an extreme-ly important decision. The future of our (country) may depend on your decision today and the unique opportunity presented to us.

A representative of the (United Nations' Special Fund) has today in-formed me that due to bureaucratic oversight there is (US$10,000,000) which has not been allocated in the budget for any specific project and which is available for the use (of Malaysia) provided that you can make a rapid decision on allocation of those funds and inform (the Secretary General of the United Nations in New York) by this afternoon. We have an open tele-phone line to (the Secretary General's Office) to notify him as soon as a decision is made. The representative apologized for the urgency of his re-quest but the fiscal year for the (United Nations) ends tonight and all funds already appropriated but not allocated to specific projects by that time will revert to the (United Nations General Fund) and will not be available for (Special Fund).

For the sake of speed and the fair allocation of the money, special representatives (from the various state assemblies of Malaysia) have been called together today to draw up a specific allocation of the money. The (United Nations) does not care how the money is allocated but (for the sake of national unity and the good of the whole country) they stipulate absolute-ly that you must come to a unanimous agreement on your decision within the time limit or lose the money.

(The United Nations) agrees to abide by whatever allocations you un-animously decide on within the next (ninety minutes).

You are already divided into your (six State Assembly) groupings:

1. Sarawak-Sabah
2. Perak-Penang-Province Wellesley
3. Kelantan-Trengganu
4. Pahang-Johore
5. Negri Sembilan-Malacca
6. Kedah-Perlis

For the sake of a speedy decision, each group will select its own negotiator and the (six) negotiators will carry out the actual negotiations on allocation of the money.

Because only (two hours) can be allowed to reach a conclusion, we have established a timetable which must be rigidly adhered to. You will have adequate time to express the proposal of your delegation, to present your proposal to the group, and to negotiate privately as well as publicly with other delegations toward unanimous agreement. While the actual nego-tiations will take place through your elected negotiator, you may, if the majority of the delegation is dissatisfied with his performance, replace your representative with someone else selected by the majority of your delegation.

Your timetable is as follows:

1. (20 minutes):   Each delegation will meet together and settle among them-selves (a) who will be the negotiator representing them in the negotiations; (b) and draw up specific plans for how the entire ($10,000,000) ought to be divided and allocated according to the needs of the entire (country) and the special concerns of your own (constituency).

2. (18 minutes):   In the first Negotiation Session, each representative will be given three minutes to report on how his delega-tion proposes to allocate the money. There will be no discussion among the representatives but each representa-tive will be given opportunity to explain the merits of his delegation's allocation of the money to the assembled company.

3. 10 minutes: In the first consultation, representatives will go back

to their own delegation for 10 minutes to consult with
them on strategy, presentation, any changes in their
proposals they may want to make,and private consultation
with members of other groups.

4. (10 minutes): In the second Negotiation Session, representatives will
present any modifications which may have been made on the
basis of having heard the other representatives' proposals
or on the basis of the consultations which have just taken
place.

5. 10 minutes: In the second consultation, further modifications in each
group's proposals can be made. Also, this is the time
to consult again with other groups on any private compro-
mises which may be proposed to secure their cooperation.

6. 20 minutes: In the third Negotiation Session, representatives will
discuss and present their final and presumably unanimously agreed upon proposal on allocation of the ($10,000,000).

Adapted from "Lump-Sum: A Bargaining Simulation Game Design," by Professor
Marshall R. Singer and Dr. Paul B. Pedersen, Kuala Lumpur, Malaysia, 1970.

---

(44)   ROLE PLAYING EMOTIONS

OBJECTIVE

To explicate how similar emotions are expressed differently or similarly across different cultures.

PARTICIPANTS

Any number of persons representing a variety of cultures who are familiar enough with one another to not be self-conscious. Facilitator.

MATERIALS

None.

SETTING

Enough open space to allow participants to engage in desired pantomime
activity.

TIME

Variable; depending on group size, length of pantomimes, and process-ing phase.

PROCEDURE

1) The facilitator will ask for volunteers to pantomime a particular emotion.

2) Each volunteer or person assigned will then select the emotions of em-barrassment, anger, fear, hate, envy, etc.

3) The members will then pantomime that emotion to the group.

4) Group members will be asked to guess what emotion he is acting out.

5) Discussion follows in regard to how emotions are expressed and inter-preted similarly or differently across different cultures.

Developed by Paul Pedersen, University of Minnesota.

---

(45) THE MOST MEMORABLE EXPERIENCE OF YOUR CHILDHOOD

OBJECTIVE

To increase cross-culture group members' ability to trust one another about half-way through a group meeting when members are starting to share important information with one another.

PARTICIPANTS

Three or more persons. Facilitator.

MATERIALS

None.

SETTING

No special requirement.

TIME

Variable.

PROCEDURE

1) Each member is asked to identify one incident from his or her own child-hood that seems particularly meaningful to them. If possible, the ear-liest memory would be most valuable.

2) Each member is asked to share that memory of his childhood with the rest of the group.

3) The group can then discuss differences in what was important for each member of the group.

Developed by Paul Pedersen, University of Minnesota.

---

(46) THE MULTICULTURAL PERSON

OBJECTIVE

We belong to many groups which function in ways similar to cultures and define our individuality in multicultural terms. This exercise was used to teach primary school children the many groups to which they belong beyond nationality or ethnic differences which define them as individuals. It attempts to teach the notion of differences in a neutral framework without evaluating those differences in terms of good or bad criteria.

PARTICIPANTS

Moderate to large group of multi-ethnic intermediate school children. Their teachers or other school personnel should be present to conduct the exercise and to help interpret its meaning.

MATERIALS

None.

SETTING

An average size school classroom provides sufficient room to accommo-date the exercise. Tables and chairs should be moved to one side or a corner of the room. The exercise may be somewhat noisy.

TIME

Variable. At least twenty minutes to a half-hour.

PROCEDURE

The exercise should follow a lecture or class discussion about prejudice, discrimination or problems persons from some cultures have experienced as a result of being different.

1) The teacher informs students that they are to move their chairs off to one side of the room to clear a large area in the center of the floor.

2) The students are then instructed to assemble in a large group in the center of the floor.

3) A list of neutral characteristics which would be likely to divide the group has been drawn up beforehand in a series of sets. They may include characteristics such as: black shoes/brown shoes/other colored shoes; those wearing red/those not wearing red; those with a penny/ those without a penny; and other similarly neutral categories.

4) The teacher reads out instructions such as: "All those wearing red move to the right side of the room and all those not wearing red move to the left side of the room." The "team" that assembles first "wins" that set. Then the group re-assembles in the center of the floor and a second set begins with the teacher reading off instructions that will divide the group in a series of ways.

5) After the group has become familiar with the exercise, the teacher may want to move toward other differences that are more personal such as hair color, eye color, tall/short, or other characteristics of the individuals.

6) Finally the teacher may want to end the exercise by using the more obviously cultural differences such as sex, national background, race, etc.

7) The discussion could center around racial/cultural differences being just one of the significant components of our individuality that define us but should not be used to evaluate our worth. The discussion might center on the role of competition both in the game, where the students were on different teams for each set, or in real life where persons who are different struggle against one another. The students might be encouraged to share incidents of how they have experienced "differentness" in themselves and in others.

Designed by Paul Pedersen, University of Minnesota.

COMMUNITY INTERACTION

(47) AMERICAN STUDIES EXERCISE

OBJECTIVE

To involve persons in an exploration of knowledge about their own culture which they feel would be most useful to them in other cultures of interest; and to consider questions and attitudes they feel they might encounter in those cultures.

PARTICIPANTS

Any number of small groups whose members are interested in functioning effectively in another culture. It is recommended that some participants be from the cultures of interest or at least be quite knowledgeable about them. Facilitator.

MATERIALS

Paper and pencils.

SETTING

No special requirements.

TIME

Variable. At least one to two hours.

PROCEDURE

1) Participants are asked to meet in groups to attempt to predict the kinds of questions they should be prepared to answer in the culture(s) of interest. Participants are also asked to focus on answers or ways of responding to these questions.

2) Paper and pencils are provided the groups, and results of each group discussion are recorded for distribution to all participants.

3) When every one has had an opportunity to read the reports from the different groups, a general community discussion or mixed small group dialogue should be conducted. The resources of the entire group can be drawn upon in exploring answers to the various questions. Each participant should, on the basis of these discussions, assess his own knowledge of American studies, his preparedness to answer the kinds of questions he could expect to encounter, and formulate his own plan of action to obtain the information he feels he should have.

4) Books and reading materials should be available for outside, individual reading.

Adapted from "American Studies Exercise" in Guidelines for Peace Corps Cross-Cultural Training, 1970. Albert R. Wight and Mary Anne Hammons, eds.

---

(48) NO QUESTIONS ASKED

OBJECTIVE

To get participants to abandon their previously learned categories of relevance, and see all of their surroundings as possibly offering clues to the nature of the community in which they find themselves.

PARTICIPANTS

Three or more persons. Facilitator.

MATERIALS

Notebook for each participant.

SETTING

1) One large room or several adjoining rooms to accommodate participants for pre-exercise briefing and follow-up discussion.

2) A community which all participants are relatively unfamiliar with.

TIME

At least one day.

PROCEDURE

1) As this exercise is designed to be 'free-form' and thereby difficult to control, it requires that the facilitator have a good knowledge of the community and be alert to any errors in observation.

2) Participants should be sent into the community for at least one afternoon with instructions to learn as much about it as possible without asking direct questions - preferably without asking questions at all.

3) This should be followed by group discussions in which the facilitator asks specific questions about the community.

Developed by Paul Pedersen, University of Minnesota.

(49) THE CULTURAL TREASURE HUNT

OBJECTIVE

To understand the behavior, values, and way of life of persons of another culture through learning about the cultural significance of items used by those persons.

PARTICIPANTS

Three or more persons. Facilitator.

MATERIALS

None required.

SETTING

1) A community that represents a culture which is unfamiliar to the majority of participants.

2) Any meeting place where free discussion can be held.

TIME

An afternoon or weekend.

PROCEDURE

1) The leader draws up short lists, each containing different items to be found within the unfamiliar community. These items might be certain kinds of local medicine, items related to religion, recreation, food, household supplies and decoration, literature, cosmetics, music, commerce -- each of which defines, in a small way, the people's behavior, values, and way of life.

2) Participants should, under most circumstances, carry out their hunt alone. They are asked to learn as much as they can about how the item is used, so that they can demonstrate its use to others when they return home.

3) When the participants are brought together again, they share the items and explain to each other what they have learned about their cultural importance. They also compare various experiences involved in carrying out the hunts -- amusing incidents, cultural differences, hostile reactions, unexpected discoveries.

4) It is very useful if there are members of the learning group who come from the "unfamiliar community," who can assist in explaining to the others about the culture of the "treasures."

Adapted from "The Cultural Treasure Hunt" in A Manual of Teaching Techniques for Intercultural Education, (UNESCO), October, 1971. Henry Holmes and Stephen Guild, eds.

(50) COMMUNITY DESCRIPTION EXERCISE

OBJECTIVE

To provide persons who will work in a culture different from their own experience with problems and difficulties, as well as rewards and satisfactions, they may expect to encounter.

PARTICIPANTS

Three or more persons. Facilitator.

MATERIALS

Paper, pencils. Descriptions of hypothetical countries.

SETTING

No special requirements.

TIME

Variable.

PROCEDURE

1) A description of a hypothetical country is written up by the facilitator, or some other source, to sound as if participants are volunteers replacing one that has completed his term of service in the area and he is describing it to them. Descriptions should be analogous to the culture of concern and provide information pertinent and useful to participants.

2) Participants read the description and complete the following on paper provided them:

   a. From the description, list those problems with which you would be most concerned as a Volunteer.

   b. From your list, select those ten problems which you consider to be the most crucial. Rank order these by placing the most crucial first, the next most crucial second, etc.

   c. Indicate what you would do about each of these ten crucial problems, considering your role as the volunteer, how you would be involved, what action you would take, etc.

Please write your name at the top of every answer sheet that you use.

3) Participants then meet in groups and develop a list of ten problems that the group as a whole feels are most important or crucial and with which the volunteer should be most concerned.

4) As a group, rank order the problems listed and indicate what action you as a group feel the Volunteer should take in respect to each of these problems.

5) Finally, the groups report out to all participants actions or solutions decided upon.

Adapted from "Community Description Exercise" in Guidelines for Peace Corps Cross-Cultural Training, 1970. Albert R. Wight and Mary Anne Hammons, eds.

---

(51) COMMUNITY EXPOSURE

OBJECTIVE

To help people develop an initial awareness of another culture by introducing them to a few fundamental cultural differences and to generate motivation to learn more about the unfamiliar culture and about themselves.

PARTICIPANTS

Three or more persons. Facilitator.

MATERIALS

Notebook, pencils.

SETTING

A community that represents a subculture different from the participants' culture.

TIME

One to three days.

PROCEDURE

1) The facilitator makes initial contact with the host communities, by visiting with their leaders and explaining the purposes of the field visit. He should offer the communities some benefits in return for hosting the group members, such as tutoring sessions which might be provided at a later date by the visitors, help in sports or recreational activities, or volunteer labor projects of public interest. For this early visit, group members should be given instructions which are brief and general, such as the following:
"Assuming you were to be sent to live in this community for several months, what do you think you would need to learn in order to make the best use of that experience?" In addition, the members receive the facilitator's telephone number and those of the key community members, in

case of emergency. Before departing for the communities, participants should be given a short time to discuss with each other their plans for carrying out the field visit.

2) It is usually most effective if participants are asked to find their way to the communities alone, or, under special circumstances, in pairs. They should be encouraged to locate accommodation in private homes. And above all, they should be asked to keep a journal of their experiences, especially taking note of any cultural differences they might observe.

3) As soon as possible after returning from the visits, the members should be convened to discuss their experiences. Any delay in the follow-up session wastes valuable momentum. The discussions should ideally be in groups of five or six. The facilitator may offer a number of questions for the members to work on, as they attempt to share and summarize their experiences.

a. Unusual physical features you noticed about the community,
b. Cultural differences you noticed between members of the community and yourself,
c. Instances in which you felt particularly "at home" during your visit,
d. Instances in which you felt particularly uncomfortable,
e. What you would need to learn in order to live usefully in the same community for several months,
f. How we can help you, in this inter-cultural education program, to function effectively in a community like this.

Adapted from "Community Exposure" in A Manual of Teaching Techniques for Intercultural Education (UNESCO), October, 1971. Henry Holmes and Stephen Guild, eds.

(52) COMMUNITY EXPLORATION

OBJECTIVE

To explore cultural characteristics of a community in some detail.

PARTICIPANTS

Three or more persons. Facilitator.

MATERIALS

Notebook, pencils.

SETTING

A community that represents a subculture different from the participants' culture.

TIME

Up to one week.

PROCEDURE

1) Group members should be encouraged to propose their own tasks and work in groups to develop their research methodologies. In fact, it is an extremely valuable task for group members to formulate their own topical "guide for understanding the community". From such an inventory, individuals can select topics to explore in detail during the field visit. The facilitator may also want to acquaint individual members with two excellent inventories of cultural topics - Murdock, et.al., Outline of Cultural Materials (1961) or Sister Inez Hilger's Field Guide to the Ethnological Study of Child Life. New Haven: Human Relations Area Files, 1966.

2) In other respects, the procedure is similar to the one described in "Community Exposure". If the group contains members who come from various host communities, these members can act as guides to one another in visits to more than one area. During the discussions following such visits, the "visitors" may be asked to describe particular features of the community; the "guides" may then evaluate the visitors' analysis.

3) To explore the feelings which the participants experienced, a useful technique is to have them draw, in retrospect, a time chart of "highs and lows" for the week. The facilitator asks them to draw up a simple calendar in which they jot down particular moments when they felt either in harmony or out of harmony with the host community. This provides ample material for discussion.

4) The facilitator should assist individual members in grouping and organizing their data.

Adapted from "Community Exploration" in A Manual of Teaching Techniques for Intercultural Education, (UNESCO), October, 1971. Henry Holmes and Stephen Guild, eds.

(53) COMMUNITY INVOLVEMENT AND SOCIAL SERVICE

OBJECTIVE

To consider a community from the perspective of social and economic change and to understand one's own problems in introducing change as an outsider who offers some social service to another society.

PARTICIPANTS

Three or more persons. Facilitator.

MATERIALS

Notebooks, pencils.

SETTING

A community that represents a subculture different from the participants' culture.

TIME

Two weeks to several months.

PROCEDURE

1) Arrangements should be made -- ideally by the participants themselves -- to provide some voluntary service to the host community in return for the field experiences; the facilitator can offer essential support and teaching assistance by being closely informed about participants' intellectual and emotional development. If he has good relationships with community leaders,he can gain valuable information about how community members view participants. Each participant should keep a careful journal which addresses at least the following topics:

a. Examples of how the community initiates or responds to social change,
b. Experiences and problems related to giving and receiving assistance,
c. Areas where his values, living style, behavior, differ from others,
d. Examples of particularly comfortable situations or particularly uncomfortable ones,
e. Notes on the particular cultural project chosen,
f. Changes the participant has experienced in his own attitude.

2) As he plans the discussion and analyses which follow the field experience, the facilitator should consider the following topics for participants to recount:

a. Different ways of scouting and entering a community, and principles of successful entry,
b. Methods of developing rapport with hosts,
c. Ways of initiating and gaining approval for the service project, and how support was obtained. Examples (and principles) of successful

and unsuccessful project development,
d. One's impact on his community, and how one can gauge and interpret this impact,
e. Examples of how members concluded their projects and left the community. This is a particularly important topic, often neglected, involving questions of manners and ethics.

3) At the end of such a long period in the community,one useful instrument to help participants evaluate their own cross-cultural progress is a "social interaction test". A simple device, it provides a format whereby participants can examine their actual social contacts in relation to their own stated values.

   a. The facilitator asks each group member to write down the names of everyone who has visited his residence on a social basis during the past month. Next he asks each one to list the names of every person whose residence he has visited. Then he asks the members to write, beside each name, the cultural group to which the name belongs. The facilitator asks the members to analyze, in terms of their own values, what patterns the list indicates to them. He may gain best results by not asking to examine the participants' lists himself saying, in effect, "These are only for your benefit, to help you look at and evaluate the way you spend your free time. If the pattern you see doesn't suit you, you may want to change it."
   b. Finally, he asks for volunteers from the group to tell the others what patterns they have found in their own social life.

Adapted from "Community Involvement and Social Service" in A Manual of Teaching Techniques for Intercultural Education (UNESCO), October, 1971. Henry Holmes and Stephen Guild, eds.

(54) TWO AUDIO-VISUAL APPROACHES

I. A Day in the Life . . . . ..

OBJECTIVE

To gain firsthand knowledge of the actual daily life of a member of another culture, once general information about the culture has been obtained.

PARTICIPANTS

Any number of two-person teams. Facilitator.

MATERIALS

Instamatic cameras; cassette tape-recorders or notebooks and pencils.

SETTING

A community that represents a subculture different from the participants' culture.

TIME

Two days.

PROCEDURE

1) The emphasis or focus of this weekend or vacation project might be one of several:

   a. A pure community description
   b. A study of an individual resident's feelings about how his own school and/or community relates to the largest society
   c. A description of the daily activities and interactions of a single person -- perhaps an older person, a local policeman, or a student of about the same age as the participant.

2) Working in two-man teams, one participant might undertake to accompany and interview a local resident, chosen according to the general subject he is pursuing. The participant records his impressions on a tape-recorder, notebook, or simply relies on his memory, depending on which seems most appropriate to the circumstances. The other participant, possibly working separately, may take slide impressions of what he perceives to be the environment in which the resident lives.

3) After editing both interview and slide materials, the evidence may be presented to the entire group. Through the selection of material in editing, and skillful discussion of their impressions following the showing, the participants are likely to develop considerable insight into the community and the meaning of their own personal experience.

4) Facilitators need to consider laying carefully the groundwork for participants' entry into this unfamiliar culture.

5) It is of utmost importance to allow the group members time to discuss the meaning of the taped-filmed experience in relation to the aims of the intercultural program.

II. Slide-Tape Essays about Foreign Persons:

OBJECTIVE

To provide a framework whereby some friendly and educational relationships can develop between persons of different cultures.

PARTICIPANTS

Any number of persons from at least two different cultures.

MATERIALS

Cameras, cassette recorders, paper and pencils.

SETTING

No special requirements.

TIME

Variable; according to preparation and presentation involvements.

PROCEDURE

1) Two persons from the same culture, using camera and cassette recorder, prepare and edit an "essay" about persons from a different culture. At least one group member should represent the culture of interest. The persons preparing the essay may concentrate in their interviews on such topics as family life, education, work and social relationships; all in the foreign and native environments. A recording may be made of the foreign person speaking (or several voices in discussion), and put together with photographed scenes of his daily life, his associations and physical surroundings. This combination of media can be extremely effective in introducing to participants an impression of a foreign person's life in another culture, as well as differences, problems and opportunities.

2) Following an editing of their material, the participants may present it to the group in several possible ways, depending on time, group composition and interests:

   a. Group members are asked to write down two words which come first to mind, in reaction to each of the first ten to twelve slides. Once the slides are complete, a discussion can follow in which the participants share, on a voluntary basis, their words and their interpretations. Much can be learned from the differing cultural perceptions of natives and foreigners.

b. Play the taped interview, either by itself or in sequence with the slides. Engage, then, in a discussion of any additional issues which have appeared from hearing the interview.

c. If the group is large, reorganize it into small interest groups, with one or two persons from different cultural backgrounds in each. This gives participants a chance to explore informally and in some depth any interests which they may have developed during the session.

Adapted from "Two Audio-Visual Approaches" in A Manual of Teaching Techniques for Intercultural Education (UNESCO), October, 1971. Henry Holmes and Stephen Guild, eds.

---

(55) WORLD PICTURE TEST

OBJECTIVE

To clarify participants' understanding of countries and cultures of the world through their knowledge of geography.

PARTICIPANTS

Three or more persons. Facilitator.

MATERIALS

Paper and pens.

SETTING

No special requirements.

TIME

At least thirty minutes to one hour.

PROCEDURE

1) Each participant is given a sheet of paper and a pen and asked to:

a. draw a map of the world as best they can within a five minute time period
b. name as many of the countries as they can
c. checkmark any country they have visited for a week or longer

    d.   exchange papers with other members of the group and discuss what differences are evidenced in what the other person put into their drawing and/or left out of the drawing.

2) Discuss the following points:

    a.   Does a person's awareness of the shape of a country reveal that person's awareness of the shape of the culture?
    b.   When a person leaves out a country, what does this mean?
    c.   When a person leaves out a continent what does this mean?
    d.   What country did the person place in the center of the map and what does that mean?
    e.   When a person draws a country out of place in relation to other countries, what does this mean?
    f.   Were they better acquainted with countries they had visited?
    g.   When the person objects violently to doing the drawing, what does that mean?
    h.   How well did persons draw home countries of other group members?
    i.   What do the persons plan to do as a result of what they learned in this exercise?

Developed by Paul Pedersen, University of Minnesota.

BRAINSTORMING TASKS AND PROBLEMS

(56)   CREATIVE PROBLEM SOLVING: AN APPROACH FOR SMALL GROUPS

OBJECTIVE

To maximize small cross-culture group problem-solving ability.

PARTICIPANTS

One or more small groups. Facilitator.

MATERIALS

Pencils and writing surfaces.

SETTING

No special requirements.

TIME

At least thirty to forty-five minutes.

PROCEDURE

1) Within fifteen minutes participants in each group are to list fifty ways to solve a given problem.

   A. Ground Rules:

       1. Do not judge or criticize suggestions with "killer phrases".
       2. Don't screen out wild or impossible ideas.
       3. Use "brainstorming" to build on one another's ideas.
       4. Adapt ideas from other problems and/or solutions.
       5. Modify the meaning, color, motion, sound, order, form or shape.
       6. Magnify the time, frequency, strength, height, length, value.
       7. Reduce to make smaller, lower, shorter, lighter.
       8. Substitute someone, something, process, power, place.
       9. Rearrange components, pattern layout, sequence, schedule.
      10. Combine, blend, ally, the assortment of purposes.

2) After the fifteen-minute time limit, group members are to evaluate and define solutions.

   A. Ground Rules: Rank all the suggestions according to the criteria listed below. Assign a (3) to the best suggestions, a (2) to the moderately good suggestions and (1) to the less useful suggestions according to each criterion. Add up the scores for each criterion.

Those suggestions with higher scores should prove most useful.

3) The facilitator leads a discussion between groups to compare scores and solutions.

SUGGESTED SOLUTIONS			INEXPENSIVE	FAST	FUN TO DO	PRACTICAL	APPROPRIATE	EASY TO DO	TOTAL SCORE
1.									
2.									
3.									
4.									
5.									
6.									
7.									
8.									
9.									
10.									
11.									
12.									
13.									
14.									
15.									
16.									
17.									
18.									
19.									
20.									

SUGGESTED SOLUTIONS			INEXPENSIVE	FAST	FUN TO DO	PRACTICAL	APPROPRIATE	EASY TO DO	TOTAL SCORE
21.									
22.									
23.									
24.									
25.									
26.									
27.									
28.									
29.									
30.									
31.									
32.									
33.									
34.									
35.									
36.									
37.									
38.									
39.									
40.									
41.									
42.									
43.									

SUGGESTED SOLUTIONS		INEXPENSIVE	FAST	FUN TO DO	PRACTICAL	APPROPRIATE	EASY TO DO	TOTAL SCORE
44.								
45.								
46.								
47.								
48.								
49.								
50.								
51.								
52.								
53.								
54.								
55.								
56.								

Developed by Paul Pedersen, University of Minnesota.

(57)   FORCE FIELD ANALYSIS

OBJECTIVE

To isolate forces that contribute to decision-making behavior in a cross-culture setting, and to acquire an appreciation of the complexity of those forces.

PARTICIPANTS

Moderate to large size groups with members of diverse cultural backgrounds. Facilitator.

MATERIALS

Paper and pencils, blackboard and chalk.

SETTING

No special requirements.

TIME

At least thirty to forty-five minutes.

PROCEDURE

1) The facilitator and/or participants select an issue pertinent to the group's dynamics or orientation, e.g. 'talking in group.'

2) Participants are then formed into culturally homogeneous small groups.

3) Each group is given a sheet of paper and a pencil.

4) The facilitator asks participants to brainstorm 'forces for' and 'forces against' talking in group. One member of each group is asked to record suggestions under the respective headings.

5) Each group is asked to read its list to the other groups. Each group's list may be reproduced on a blackboard for comparison and discussion purposes.

Adapted from "Force Field Analysis" in <u>Guidelines for Peace Corps Cross-Cultural Training</u>, 1970. Albert R. Wight and Mary Anne Hammons, eds.

MULTIPLE OBJECTIVES

(58) POINTS TO CONSIDER

OBJECTIVE

To derive optimal value from a cross-cultural encounter.

PARTICIPANTS

One or more persons.

MATERIALS

None.

SETTING

No special requirements.

TIME

At least five to ten minutes.

PROCEDURE

1) Examine the following eleven points in preparation for an upcoming cross-cultural encounter.

2) Discuss with other involved persons the implications of each point.

To derive value from the cross-cultural encounter:

1. Examine your habitual behavior for their communication content.

2. Question the absoluteness of your values and premises.

3. Recognize the other person's anxieties and his need to preserve his cultural identity.

4. Admit your own insecurities in the face of an unknown foreign quantity.

5. Listen to what the other person is communicating, not to what is going on in your own head.

6. Seek to detach your ego from its cultural reinforcements sufficiently to be able to express honestly your true feelings.

7. Try to use descriptive terms rather than those expressing approval or disapproval.

8. Try to use phrases to which you have given thorough consideration.

9. Try to move in the direction of substituting more precise words for vague ones.

10. Become more alert to the ways in which cultural conditioning shapes one's value judgements.

11. Become more suspicious of one's own "wisdom."

---

(59) CULTURALLY MIXED GROUPS

OBJECTIVE

To enable persons to have an open, honest, meaningful encounter with a person from another culture.

PARTICIPANTS

Any number of groups of eight to ten persons, each group representing at least two cultures. Facilitator.

MATERIALS

Use of questionnaires to facilitate collection and analysis of data is recommended.

SETTING

No special requirements.

TIME

Variable. Several hour-long group meetings recommended.

PROCEDURE

1) Once the culturally mixed groups are assembled, members are assigned the tasks of:

   a. getting to know one another,
   b. identifying differences between cultures and possible areas of con-

flict,
c. exploring various ways of achieving increased understanding, harmony, and unity.

2) The facilitator should not be present in the group. It then becomes the responsibility of the group to develop itself into a cohesive, working, achieving group and to solve problems as they develop.

3) Discussion Group questionnaires may be used to facilitate collection and analysis of data. Data can be consolidated and fed back in many ways, but it is useful to focus on differences in perceptions and responses of the two groups.

Adapted from "Culturally Mixed Groups" in Guidelines for Peace Corps Cross-Cultural Training, 1970. Albert R. Wight and Mary Anne Hammons, eds.

REFERENCES ON ADDITIONAL CROSS-CULTURAL EXERCISES

AFS Program Development Department. AFS Orientation Handbook,
Vols. 1-5. New York, NY: AFS International/Intercultural
Programs, 1981-1985.

Batchelder, Donald and Elizabeth G. Warner. Beyond Experience,
The Experiential Approach to Cross-Cultural Education. Brattle-
boro, VT: The Experiment in International Living. 1977.

Ferguson, Henry. Manual for Multicultural Education. Yarmouth,
ME: Intercultural Press, Inc. 1986.

Fersch, Seymour. Learning About Peoples and Cultures.
Evanston, IL: McDougall, Littell & Co. 1974.

Hoopes, David S. and Paul Ventura, eds. Intercultural
Sourcebook: Cross-Cultural Training Methodologies. Yarmouth,
ME: Intercultural Press, Inc. 1979.

Kohls, L. Robert. Developing Intercultural Awareness.
Washington, D.C.: SIETAR, 1981.

McCune, S.M., C. Greaser and R. Blecker. Simulation and Games
(an international journal of theory, design and research).
Beverly Hills, CA: Sage. Issues beginning in 1970.

Otero, George G. Teaching About Perception: The Arabs. Denver,
CO: CTIR, University of Denver. 1977.

Pfeiffer, J., W. Jones and J.E. Jones (eds.). The Annual
Handbook for Group Facilitators. LaJolla, CA: University
Associates. 1972 to present.

Pusch, Margaret D., ed. Multicultural Education: A Cross-
Cultural Training Approach. Yarmouth, ME: Intercultural Press,
Inc. 1986.

Renwick, George W. Evaluation Handbook for Cross-Cultural
Training and Multicultural Education. Yarmouth, ME: Intercultural Press, Inc. 1979.

Ruben, Brent and Richard W. Budd. Human Communication Handbook: Simulations and Games. Rochelle Park, NJ: Hayden Book
Co., Inc. 1975.

Seelye, H. Ned. Teaching Culture. Skokie, IL: National
Textbook Co. 1984.

Sikkema, Mildred and Agnes Niyekawa. Design for Cross-
Cultural Learning. Yarmouth, ME: Intercultural Press,
Inc. 1986.

Smith, Gary R. and George G. Otero. Teaching About Cultural
Awareness. Denver, CO: CTIR, University of Denver. 1977.